CREATING
BONSAI
LANDSCAPES

CREATING
BONSAI
LANDSCAPES

Su Chin Ee

STOREY

A QUARTO BOOK

Published by Storey Publishing, 2003
210 MASS MoCA Way
North Adams, MA 01247

The mission of Storey Publishing is to serve our customers by publishing practical information that encourages personal independence in harmony with the environment.

Library of Congress Cataloging-in-Publication Data
Ee, Su Chin
    Creating bonsai landscapes: 18 miniature garden
    projects/by Su Chin Ee.
    p. cm.
    ISBN 1–58017–484–1 (alk. paper)
    1. Bonsai. I. Title
SB433.5.E342003
635.9772–dc21

QUAR.BOST

Conceived, designed, and produced by
Quarto Publishing plc
The Old Brewery
6 Blundell St
London N7 9BH

Project Editors Tracie Lee Davis, Fiona Robertson
Art Editor Karla Jennings
Designer Caroline Grimshaw
Text Editors Jan Cutler, Karen Levy, Stephanie Chilman
Assistant Art Director Penny Cobb
Photographer Paul Forrester
Illustrators Kuo Kang Chen, Julian Baker
Proofreader Anne Plume
Indexer Pamela Ellis

Art Director Moira Clinch
Publisher Piers Spence

Storey books are available for special premium and promotional uses and for customized editions. For further information, please call Storey's Custom Publishing Department at 1–800–793–9396.

Manufactured by
Pica Digital Pte Ltd, Singapore
Printed by
Leefung Asco Printers Ltd., China

9 8 7 6 5 4 3 2 1

CONTENTS

FOREWORD

When I first saw Su Chin's work, back in 1983, I was immediately struck by her obvious love of nature and her sense of landscape. Even her single-tree plantings had a particular charm that was not apparent in the work of other bonsai artists. During the years that followed we became firm friends, and I began to understand where this special magic came from.

Although Su Chin was brought up in Singapore, she did not discover bonsai as a creative discipline until she had moved to England to study art. Her Chinese heritage, her natural artistic skills, and the westernized version of bonsai, which was taught in England at that time, formed a unique combination that developed into an accessible approach to capturing the natural beauty of trees and landscapes in miniature. Why accessible? Another of Su Chin's attributes is her ability to inspire and instruct her western students, regardless of their horticultural or artistic skills. Her enthusiasm and generosity of spirit have guided many along the road to creating their own magical and mystic landscapes, leading to endless pleasure as these miniature masterpieces mature and change with the passing seasons.

With Su Chin there is no repetition of concept, no recourse to a design formula; everything she does is original and infused with the timeless mysticism of ancient China. Su Chin's attitude is pragmatic: her comprehensive horticultural knowledge, her understanding of the western mind, and her down-to-earth practical approach make her students instantly aware that they, too, can create equally charming scenes with plants and materials that can be found easily in local stores and garden centres.

Learning the art of bonsai landscapes from Su Chin Ee requires no coaching in Oriental spiritualism, no complicated horticultural techniques, and no investment in expensive tools or materials. All that is required is a love of nature and the ability to sit back, close your eyes, and imagine.

COLIN LEWIS

Colin Lewis is the author of several books on bonsai including the best-selling *Bonsai Survival Manual* (Storey, 1996). He is also Consulting Editor of *Bonsai* magazine, and conducts seminars throughout Europe and the United States to teach the craft of bonsai.

This book is a thank you to Madam Magdeleine Sim and Madam Deanna Wong. To you both, for giving me such a gift of beauty and creation.

And to all who have believed in and appreciated my work.

INTRODUCTION

My landscapes represent a very personal synthesis of the bonsai and *penjing* traditions, with influences drawn from my life as a painter in the West. My journey toward creating miniaturized landscapes began at London's Royal College of Art. There, through my painting, I imagined myself to be a scholar creating miniature gardens from times gone by. I was fortunate to meet many accomplished bonsai artists who helped me understand the ancient Chinese art of *penjing*, or "landscape in a pot or dish," and I am grateful to them for passing on their knowledge to me. I incorporate bonsai trees and shrubs into my landscapes—bonsai meaning "pot tree" in Japanese. I also found inspiration in the formal order of topiary and in the old sinks and troughs planted with tiny alpine specimens that I had seen in Western gardens.

My work has been considered controversial because I approach my landscapes from the point of view of a painter. I concentrate on delicate variations of color, shading, and light, using the vegetation to add tone and bring the scene to life. When I create a miniature landscape, I intend it to be a means of transporting myself to an imaginary place of mountains and water. As I have gained confidence over the years, I have learned how to create a true representation of a natural scene, using planting techniques and adding details that deceive the eye into believing there is much greater depth or height to the landscape. Handmade rocks form the basic structure for many of my landscapes. Made with chicken wire covered with ciment fondu they take on a powerful, rugged, and natural appearance as they weather and as the tiny plants creep over them, giving the miniature landscapes a sense of richness.

I also incorporate positive and negative elements, using the Chinese principles of Tao and the balance of yin and yang to give perfect harmony to my creations: old with new, masculine with feminine, and light with shade.

I hope that you will enjoy my discovery of these beautiful worlds in miniature.

SU CHIN EE

MATERIALS

You can begin with just three essential tools: a bonsai branch pruner, a pair of short-handled scissors, and a pair of long-handled scissors. Adapt garden and other tools already in your possession, and add to your bonsai kit as you gain knowledge and experience.

Improvisation is all part of the art of growing bonsai. The early Chinese, remember, produced beautiful trees long before speciality bonsai suppliers existed.

plants

▼ Plants from a nursery

Nurseries are full of potential bonsai. Look for bushy trees with low-growing branches and interesting trunks. Always keep root and foliage balanced, remove one third of branches to one third of the root ball.

▼ Cuttings

Softwood cuttings are taken from deciduous trees and hardwood cuttings from older branches and evergreens. For best results, always take cuttings from the lower portion of the tree. Keep cuttings in warm shade and spray frequently.

▼ Seedlings

Seedlings are often more vigorous than cuttings, and many varieties are quick to grow. Japanese and trident maples, black pine, Scots pine, zelkovas, beech, almond, horse chestnut, crab apple, quince, and larch are all easy subjects.

TIPS

• When buying seed, remember there is no such thing as "bonsai seed." A reputable dealer will always describe seeds as "tree seeds suitable for growing bonsai."
• If you don't have any deep seed trays, old grow bags can be used for rooting cuttings. Punch holes in the bottom for drainage and add a little sharp sand.

containers

► High quality, unglazed baked clay suiban (water tray), imported from Japan.

▲ Glass pot saucer, available at florist shops.

▲ Glazed clay tray for bonsai pots, available at garden centers.

► Half-crescent pot made by a specialist potter. The rim follows the line of a mountainous horizon.

soils and planting mediums

▼ Chick grit

Mix in with the soil for aeration. Chick grit encourages the subdivision of roots by forcing them to split. It is also used for cosmetic purposes.

▲ Akadama

Coarse, baked potting clay from Japan, akadama has to be sifted into three grades before use. Put the coarse grade at the bottom of the pot for drainage; use the medium grade for general potting; then, after planting, sprinkle the fine grade on the top to encourage moss to grow.

▼ Ericaceous soil

Acidic soil mix used mainly for azaleas. An alkaline (lime) soil mix would kill them.

▲ Bonsai soil mix

A good base formula for bonsai soil is one part loam, two parts sphagnum moss, and two parts granite grit. It should be slightly springy in texture—when squeezed in your hand it should neither crumble apart nor ooze water.

▼ Sphagnum moss

A very coarse wet florist's moss used in the air-layering propagation method. Excellent as a repair moss, it holds a lot of moisture, encourages roots, and keeps the soil aerated.

▼ Gravel

There are three grades of gravel: Coarse, used at the edges of plantings to depict big stones at the river's banks; medium, used closer to the center of the river; and fine, to depict the bed of the river.

▲ Sedge peat

Useful for making bonsai pads. When mixed with water, it forms a yogurtlike substance. Good for rhododendrons and azaleas.

▲ Leaf mold

Full of nutrients, leaf mold opens up the soil, encouraging good growth. To sterilize, place it in a microwave on full power for 2 minutes. Leave overnight before use.

moss

◀ Glazed pottery tray, made to order by a potter.

▼ Terra-cotta tray, available at garden centers, enhanced with grey slate paint.

Moss absorbs fertilizer and prevents water from reaching the soil, so it should be used sparingly. Make sure you cover no more than one third of the soil and always keep the rim of the tray clear. It should not be allowed to grow up the trunks of your bonsai. If it does, scrub it off with a small plastic brush and spray the trunk with water.

When gathering moss, look for a good soil base. This soil can be used separately to mix with the sedge peat—it is wonderfully porous, full of nutrients, and ideal for the main planting. If you buy moss, it usually comes in ¼-inch (5mm) pieces. Store it in a cool place between layers of newspaper. It will shrivel and dry but will still be alive. When you are ready to plant, awaken it by spraying with rainwater. Make sure you press the moss very firmly into the soil. To help it acclimatize, cover it with plastic for a couple of weeks.

landscaping tools and materials

▼ Sieve for akadama
For separating akadama clay into its three grades of texture before potting.

▲ Tweezers
Useful for holding delicate branches when pruning, and for removing garden debris after moving trees indoors.

▼ Gauze
Used in the same way as chicken wire, gauze has a finer mesh, so it can be coated without needing to be reinforced with fiberglass cloth.

▲ Ciment fondu
A very fine cement that sets when it comes into contact with water. Ideal for constructing original rocks. Available from building and masonry suppliers, or from a company called Lafarge.

▼ Chopsticks
Used to remove air pockets from around the roots when repotting. Any root left in an air pocket will die.

▲ Raffia
Used to wrap around delicate trunks and branches to protect them from wire damage. Available at craft stores.

▶ Metal pipe for support
Used for reinforcement when constructing rocks.

▼ String
Used to tie young, unstable trees to their pots.

▶ Chinese watercolors
Paint new pots with Chinese watercolors to give the impression of age. You can also use Windsor & Newton paints.

▲ Epoxy glue
Very strong, adaptable, waterproof puttylike glue. Used to glue wire to rocks and for anchoring trees.

▼ Chicken wire
Used with fiberglass cloth to shape ciment-fondu rocks and contain awkward root masses before final potting.

▶ Florist's wire
Cut into hairpin-shaped loops, ¼ to ½ inch (6–12mm) in size, the wire is used to pin newly planted moss onto the soil.

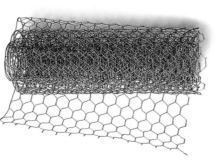

natural materials

You can gather your own pieces from the wild or buy them. The Chinese cockerel rock I used in this book was imported by a speciality shop. The natural shape of a piece of driftwood can be built up into a container with the help of sedge peat. You can buy pebbles from aquarium shops to depict pebbles on a beach. Gravel is used decoratively, rather like moss. It holds in the soil and stops water from spilling out.

▼ Plastic tubing (for water pump)
Used to feed through rock when creating a waterfall landscape. It is affixed to the pump underwater.

▼ Pump
Electric water pump with adjustable flow for waterfall styles. Small, modern pumps are now available, which means you can use shallower trays that are more aesthetically pleasing.

▼ Mixing bowl
For making ciment fondu and mixing sedge peat. A glass 3-inch (7.5cm) bowl is best.

▲ Pliers
The concave branch cutter (bottom), used for complete removal of branches, is the most useful and essential of all bonsai tools. The twig cutter (top) is used for cutting branches from inside the foliage canopy.

▲ Bonsai wire
For shaping trunks and branches. Traditional copper cable wire has been replaced by anodized aluminum as the favorite for home growers. You can also use single-core PVC or galvanized plastic-covered wire, easily found in hardware and gardening stores.

▲ Silicone glue
For affixing rocks to the water tray in waterscapes. Can be found at art and aquarium supply stores.

▲ Quick-drying cement
Used for quick repairs, for making small boulders, and for cementing rocks to the water tray.

▲ Paintbrushes
For applying ciment fondu to chicken wire and fine dusting. Also used for painting traditional backgrounds for display.

▲ Scissors
You will need a pair of short-bladed scissors (top) for cutting fine branches and twigs, leaf pruning, and probing deep into the branch structures of mature trees. A pair of long-bladed scissors (below), for root and general trimming, are also essential.

Cockerel rock

Driftwood

Pebbles

Gravel

TECHNIQUES

You will have many opportunities to use your artistic skills when you grow bonsai. Always look to nature for inspiration and clues as to how to proceed, and always keep the harmonious aesthetic of the whole in mind. Approach these techniques with as flexible and innovative a spirit as possible. As you gain experience, you will want to try some new ideas of your own.

making rocks with ciment fondu

Throughout this book, I make rocks, boulders, and other forms of landscaping using ciment fondu. Ciment fondu is available from building and masonry suppliers, and it has many qualities that are ideal for bonsai landscapes. It is easy to use: It comes as a powder that is mixed into water (use equal proportions of water and powder, and never add water to the powder), and it dries fairly quickly. It is impervious to water once it has set, is much lighter than concrete, and is frost proof. To set it, wrap it in damp newspaper and then a plastic sheet for 24 hours.

The following instructions are for a simple, bowl-shaped landscape that I planted with an artillery plant *(Pilea microphylla)* and a water fern *(Azorella filiculoides)*. The method is the same for all of the projects in the book, with the exception of Gong Ji Shan and Jin Shi.

YOU WILL NEED:

1. Gloves and mask
2. Chicken wire
3. Wire cutters
4. Fiberglass cloth
5. Needle and thread
6. Dust mask
7. Ciment fondu in gray and white
8. Mixing bowl
9. Paintbrush
10. Newspaper
11. Plastic sheet
12. Professional watercolor paints
13. Sedge peat
14. Artillery plant
15. Water fern

TIPS

• Because it sets when it comes into contact with water, never wash cement down the sink. Wrap it in newspaper and put it in the trash.
• Cement should be stored in an airtight container and kept in a cool place.

❶ Put on gloves when working with wire. Rolls of chicken wire are approximately 18 inches (45cm) wide. Cut a length 18 inches (45cm) long so that you have a square, and sew the fiberglass cloth to both sides using strong cotton thread and a large needle. Sew at approximately 1-inch (2.5cm) intervals so the fiberglass cloth is secure.

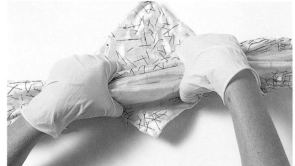

❷ Fold the wire and fiberglass square into a triangle, then begin to pleat each side, folding 2- to 3-inch sections (5 to 7.5cm) backward and forward until you have a fan effect. This pleating gives the finished construction interesting crinkles and texture, and avoids an unrealistic smooth finish.

❸ Fan out the pleating and start shaping your rock or bowl.

❹ When you are happy with the shape, put on a dust mask and mix up the ciment fondu in a small bowl. Apply it to the fiberglass cloth with a paintbrush. You will learn by experience how quickly the ciment fondu dries. It can take a couple of hours to cover your construction. I used white ciment fondu inside to reflect the water and gray ciment fondu outside to imitate rock. When you have finished, wrap the construction in damp newspaper, then cover it with a plastic sheet.

❺ Allow 24 hours for the construction to set. Rinse off any dust, and wait for it to dry. I use professional watercolor paints, which tend to be more colorfast. Mix <u>greens</u>, <u>browns</u>, and <u>purples</u>, then paint the rock, thinking of it as a mountain range. Once the paint is dry, make planting pockets in the cavities with sedge peat, and position the plants.

alternative methods of construction

Instead of chicken wire and fiberglass cloth, I sometimes use aluminum gauze and plaster gauze together. This is a very simple and quick method. You shape the aluminum gauze, wet the plaster gauze according to the label's instructions, then layer it on the aluminum. While the plaster gauze is wet, sprinkle quick-drying cement over it to achieve an instantly realistic rock. Plaster gauze, however, is not frost proof so constructions made with this method must be kept indoors.

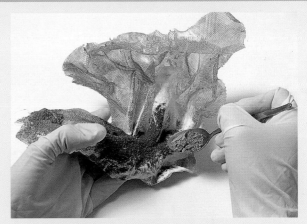

For the Jin Shi project (see page 60), I wanted a rock that would have silver lines shot through it. I covered aluminum gauze with aluminum foil to create the shape of the rock. I molded the rock with the foil on the outside, then brushed on ciment fondu. When it set, glints of silver could be seen through the rock.

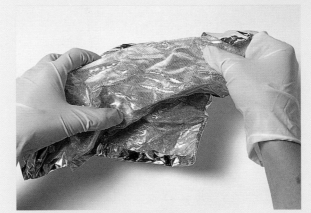

For Gong Ji Shan (see page 36), which is a very tall construction, I used metal rods to support the chicken wire. There are many household items that can be adapted for use, from coat hangers to banana hangers. You can buy very thick bonsai wire that can be shaped into a support, or metal rods can be bought from craft stores. The metal support will need to be secured to a piece of wood. Use quick-drying cement for this.

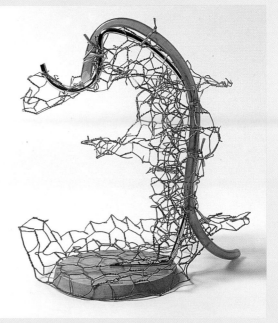

bonsai pads and planting pockets

training and moving

I create bonsai pads for my plants using the following method, which is not traditional. Many people plant the young trees in small training trays, such as a seed tray, and root prune them for 2 or 3 years, until they have strong fibrous pads and are ready to transfer to a shallow dish. The following method is simple and quick, and I find it works just as well as the traditional method.

1 On your chosen surface, build sausages of sedge peat (a water-retentive soil). Slowly add water until it becomes sticky (imagine you are making a mud pie), and mold it into a sausage shape. Make sections of sausage and create a planting pocket to surround the tree's roots and form the edges of the bonsai pad.

If a tree is to be planted on a hillside, tilt the container and support it with rocks. Continue as before, and in 48 hours the tree will have a bonsai pad that follows the angles of the planned landscape. This will make it much easier to position the tree in the landscape.

2 Remove the plant from the pot and check that its root system looks healthy. It should not be too pot-bound, but the roots should be visible around the edges of the pot. Tease out all the soil from the roots, then cut the adventitious roots (thick roots that support the tree) by one third.

3 Sprinkle coarse akadama or chick grit in the planting pocket. This will act as drainage material.

Use a spatula or cake server when moving a tree with a bonsai pad. This ensures that there is minimal disturbance to the roots.

4 Soak the roots of the tree in wet sedge peat, piling the peat onto and around the roots so that they are almost covered, then lift the roots and sedge peat with a spoon and lower them into the planting pocket.

5 Firm in the tree, squeezing the sausage edges in toward the roots so that the tree is stable.

6 The wet sedge peat will solidify and set over the next 24 to 48 hours, at which time the tree can be pruned and is ready to be transplanted into a landscape, if desired.

painting backgrounds

The projects throughout this book are offset by traditional Chinese watercolor paintings that enhance the landscapes. Although you will probably keep your bonsai landscape outdoors most of the time, you may want to display it indoors when guests visit. A painted background will set off your creation perfectly. In the following demonstration, I depict a lush mountain scene that will tower over a rock pool.

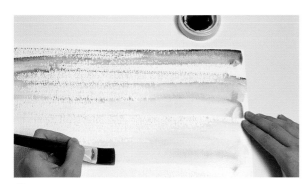

YOU WILL NEED:

1. Heavy-grade acid-free watercolor paper
2. Professional watercolor paints
3. 1-inch (2.5cm) flat brush
4. Fine (size 1) brush
5. Mixing bowl
6. Water bowl
7. Salt
8. Hairdryer

1 Ensure that your sheet of paper is larger than the landscape you are intending to display. Using a flat brush, paint a background wash, using a little paint in a large amount of water.

2 Paint the first lines of your landscape, then sprinkle some spots of paint with the end of your paintbrush. Using water, blur the lines of the landscape. Work quickly, as you will need to apply salt while the paint is still wet.

TIPS

• Use bold brushstrokes and avoid hard edges.
• Keep the subject matter in the center section of the paper, where all attention will be focused.
• For a flower effect, I like to flick paint from the brush straight onto the paper.

3 Before the paint dries, quickly sprinkle it lightly with salt, then dry it with a hairdryer. The salt absorbs some of the water from the paint and softens the colors, giving a smoky effect as well as adding an attractive sparkle and sheen in places.

4 Choose another color to define the edges of the mountains. The effect should be very impressionistic, so do not worry too much about the accuracy of your lines. Do a small amount to start, as you will again need to work on the paint before it dries.

5 Continue to build up the lines of the mountains, adding salt and then drying the paint as you proceed. Finally, when the paint is completely dry, stand the picture up and give it a very gentle shake. Excess salt will drop off the painting.

THE LANDSCAPES

Miniature landscapes are a wonderful way to create an illusion. In the following projects, you will discover how to use trees and shrubs to give the effect of distance and height. You can give the impression of trees high on a mountaintop by using tiny trees at the top of your handmade rock to contrast with larger plantings at the base.

Some of the landscapes use water to add interest and beauty to the scene. This can be a small pond, moving water flowing around the base of the landscape, or still water that will reflect the plants and rocks. Other landscapes are dry but are given the appearance of water by using graded gravel to suggest its movement. By dividing the landscape with a winding gravel "stream" that passes beneath a bridge and disappears from view, you can suggest distance.

You can replicate an entirely natural scene, perhaps using small ornamental figurines, pagodas, or bridges to add to the sense of scale, or you can create sheer fantasy with metallic rocks and beaches. You can also translate myths, as I have done, and choose plants that represent animals, such as the mighty dragon or the phoenix.

Some of my landscapes are at their best in the fall, when their leaves are golden brown. Others are a flush of vivid color as they display spring blossoms or summer flowers. Some of the larger landscapes have elements that come into play at different times of the year, providing a continually changing scene.

Most of the landscapes do best outside for the greater part of the year, as they contain hardy miniaturized trees. Occasionally, you will want to move them indoors so they can be displayed. The projects will explain how to care for each landscape so that it will thrive.

Shan Shui
MOUNTAIN WATER

The Shan Shui landscape is a portrait of heaven, and this scene appears as though seeds from above have sown the tableau. The majestic center mountain, Crane Mountain, soars like the spirit to a great height and towers above two smaller hills. As it extends upward into the sky, it increases in size. It represents a masculine yang rock flanked by two smaller yin mountains. Heavy rain and strong winds have carved a spectacular natural sculpture from these elements, and as you look at the landscape, you can almost feel and hear the wind blowing.

Turtle Mountain, on the left, represents Earth. It is named after the black turtle, an animal that was considered a protector and guardian in Japanese myth. Turtle Mountain is a safe haven and is therefore the best place to nest or build a home. The rock on the right supports the oldest tree in the landscape, which represents humankind. I used a very old triangular pattern of lines—vertical (representing heaven), horizontal (representing Earth), and diagonal (representing humanity)—to create this landscape.

I selected Japanese larch (*Larix kaempferi*) of all ages, shapes, and styles, and treated the entire vista as a single element. To enhance the sense of perspective, I planted small, slender trees at the top and larger specimens in the foreground.

setting up

◀ Metal rods for foundation
Metal rods of various widths and lengths are available from hardware stores. The rods I use are ¹⁄₁₆ inch (2mm) thick. If you need to cut them to length, use a metal saw, or ask your supplier to do the job for you.

Plastic sheeting
The sheeting is to protect your work surface and to wrap the ciment-fondu rock, so any sort can be used. I sometimes split open trash can liners and use those.

Fiberglass cloth
Fiberglass cloth is available from craft and art supply stores (it is often used to make model airplanes). Sheets of various sizes and weight are available. The type I use is 1.5 oz. per square yard.

▶ Chicken wire
Lightweight chicken wire with ½-inch (10mm) mesh is available at hardware stores.

Needle and thread
Attach the fiberglass cloth to the chicken wire with a strong sewing needle and thread.

Sedge peat
This is an ideal planting medium for bonsai landscapes. When water is added to sedge peat, it becomes sticky and can be used to create planting pockets and bonsai pads (see page 14).

▶ Bonsai wire
Copper-colored aluminum wire is available from bonsai suppliers. It is used for securing roots and branches.

Mixing bowl
You will need a mixing bowl for making ciment fondu.

Wire cutters
You will need wire cutters to cut the chicken wire.

Constructing the landscape

Start by making a sketch of your finished rocks. Spread a piece of plastic sheeting on your work surface. Wear protective gloves when working with the chicken wire and a face mask when mixing and applying the ciment fondu.

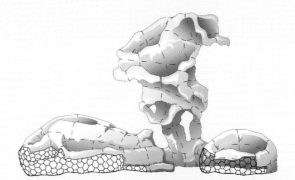

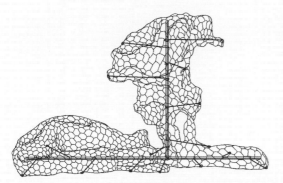

1 Select a metal rod that is as long as the full width of the base of the largest rock. The rod is necessary to strengthen the base. Thread the rod through chicken wire, which will form the desired shape of the base. Attach a second, vertical rod by threading it down through the chicken wire mesh. This will act as the main support for the tallest rock. Form the outline shape of the central rock in chicken wire, ensuring that the rod is lodged firmly in the mesh.

2 At this stage, make any alterations to the shape or other fine adjustments. Create a cavity for the rock pool. Follow the instructions on pages 12–13 for making fondu rocks, using the mixing bowl, ciment fondu, fiberglass cloth, needle, thread, paints, and brush. Once dry, the ciment fondu will hold the rod and chicken wire structure in place.

3 The smaller rocks are formed in the same way as the central rock but do not require any structural support. To create a small water basin, insert a piece of pond liner into a suitable crevice in the rock. After applying the ciment fondu (see page 13), wrap the rock in damp newspaper and plastic. Let set for 24 hours, then rinse with water.

▼ Ciment fondu
Ciment fondu is available from building and masonry suppliers; it is also used for sculpting.

Protective clothing
Wear gloves and a face mask when working with fiberglass cloth and cement.

▶ Brush
A decorator's brush, approximately 1 inch (2.5cm) wide or less, is used to apply the ciment fondu to the fiberglass cloth.

▼ Chopsticks or a thin stick
Chopsticks are the perfect implement for working soil between the roots of plants.

▶ Akadama
Akadama is a general-purpose soil imported from Japan. It contains clay granules, which give it water-retentive properties.

▶ Chinese watercolors
I use watercolor paints to add subtle tones to terra-cotta dishes and trays.

Pond liner
This is a thick plastic sheeting that does not deteriorate in water. You can buy it at garden centers.

Newspaper
Wrap the ciment-fondu rock in damp newspaper and plastic until it has set.

Planting plan

Once dry, wash your rock construction to remove surface dust. Roll sedge peat into a long sausage to form planting pockets (see page 14). In the pockets, place a shallow layer of coarse akadama to improve drainage. Place the trees, with bonsai pads, on top of the coarse akadama, then add a layer of medium akadama. Insert a chopstick vertically into the soil and twist it to work soil between the roots. Finish with a dusting of fine akadama to encourage moss to grow. Place a single larch on the right, a group of larches on the top of the tallest rock, a group to the left of the landscape, and a single larch in front of the left-hand group.

Plant the sempervivum in sedge peat at the base of the trees on each of the rocks, where its root system will help support the trees. Plant the sedum 'Cape Blanco' at the base of the right-hand rock, and the thyme to its right. Place the other sedum (*Sedum hispanicum*) on the right-hand side of the tall rock, then add moss wherever soil remains exposed to help retain moisure and enhance the coloring of the landscape. Add the azorella to exposed soil to the left of the landscape.

1. *Larix kaempferi*
2. *Sempervivum tectorum*
3. *Sedum hispanicum*
4. *Thymus serpyllum* 'Elfin'
5. Moss
6. *Sedum spathulifolium* 'Cape Blanco'
7. *Azorella trifurcata*

CARE

- **Positioning:** Place in full sun. It can be useful to place a landscape on a lazy Susan (turntable) in order to rotate it so the trees receive sun from every side.
- **Watering:** Water with a fine rose-head watering can each day. You may have to water up to 3 times a day in hot weather. Use rainwater if possible, as tap water can cause limescale to build up over time.
- **Feeding:** Feed once a month from March to October with commercially available bonsai fertilizer.
- **Pruning:** In spring, fall, and winter, allow shoots to develop until side buds swell, then pinch them back to above a side bud.

the scenery

▼ *Thymus serpyllum* 'Elfin'
I chose this thyme variety to represent low-growing foliage, because it covers a large area and helps shape the soil mix around the area where you will set the planting. Its purple-green color creates an illusion of depth. You will need one plant for the landscape.

▼ *Sedum spathulifolium* 'Cape Blanco'
The plump leaves of this sedum are useful for providing a change in ground texture. The plant covers the sides of one of the smaller hills, and the blue leaves contrast attractively with the reddish bark of the nearby larch. I used one sedum as "punctuation" at the base of the largest tree; it provides the sense of taking a breath before moving your eye to the left of the scene.

▼ *Sedum hispanicum*
Most of the alpines used here have been transplanted from gravel paths. Do this in spring, because transplanting in summer will not work and the plant will die. In spring, *Sedum hispanicum* displays a network of delicate branches that give a sense of age to the landscape. The plant also has an arid look in spring, which conjures up an image of the harsh weather in the mountains. You will need one clump for the landscape.

▼ Moss
This lush green moss plays an important part in forming a visual link between the left and right sides of the landscape; it also holds the soil mix in place for the planting. Its bright green color acts as a focal point, drawing the eye to the landscape and then to the solid rock below.

Informal upright style

The informal upright style (as opposed to the formal upright style) is the most commonly found style in bonsai. In formal upright style, the trunk should be straight and taper toward the top. In informal style, the trunk will have some curvature. There is not a fixed technique, but certain rules apply. Most species of tree are suitable for training in the informal upright style.

1 ▶ Select a 2- to 3-year-old tree from a garden center. Choose one with a thick trunk that is slightly curved and sinuous in appearance. If the trunk is straight, it can be trained in a sinuous style with wire. When you buy a garden-center tree, it will be bushy and full of branches. Your first task is to thin them out. You need to remove approximately one third of the branches so that you can clearly see the remaining ones.

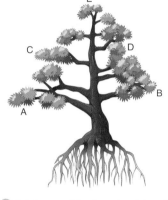

2 Cut the remaining branches into a tidy shape and select which ones will be the final branches that will be wired into shape. On this tree, (A) will be the main left branch, (B) the main right branch, (C) a back branch for depth, (D) a forward-bowing branch, and (E) the apex where the top foliage pad will form.

3 The root system will be enormous at this stage. In spring, reduce the root system by one third. Put the tree into a bonsai pot. If you plant the tree at a slight angle, you will achieve the beginning of the sinuous trunk. Allow the foliage to grow quite freely at this stage so that the trunk will thicken and age nicely.

4 Wiring shapes the trunk and trains the branches to form the foliage pads (see page 69). The tree should be roughly triangular shaped. Branches at the bottom of the tree should be longest and thickest, reducing in both length and girth as you proceed up the tree. At the apex, allow a cluster of twigs to grow to form a flat top.

5 Keep trimming the branches to encourage foliage pads to form, taking away all downward growth. After 2 years, the wires can be removed.

▼ *Sempervivum tectorum*
Many varieties of hens-and-chicks are useful for bonsai landscapes, as they form richly colored carpets of foliage. Choose one with small rosettes. I chose this one for its dull green leaves to contrast with the bright green foliage of the larches. You will need approximately six clumps for the landscape.

▶ *Larix kaempferi*
Japanese larch grows to between 80 and 100 feet (24m and 30m) tall in its natural habitat, and it is exciting to think how this large and graceful tree can be tamed to suit a bonsai landscape. All the trees in this landscape are larches trained or grown in different ways. The tree at the right of the landscape is in the informal upright style (see above), while the three groups of trees on the left and in the center are in the clump style (see page 33). You will need two single trees and three groups of trees to create this landscape.

▶ *Azorella trifurcata*
This alpine is often mistaken for a moss. Like moss, it helps hold the soil mix in place for the planting. Its color is a lovely green tinged with yellow, which contrasts with the tone of the moss. I used a single plant in this landscape to draw the eye to the left foreground, where a single larch is planted in front of the group.

Shan Shui
MOUNTAIN WATER

山
水

Ba Xian
EIGHT IMMORTALS

With the spring morning mist appearing from the heavens, eight immortals from Chinese mythology descend upon two entwined Chinese elms *(Ulmus parvifolia)* perched on two mountains. The Chinese elm is often given as a gift for Christmas or birthdays, but these two gnarled trees are older than those usually available in stores and have been styled in a more elaborate way than typical shop-bought trees.

The design concept is based on the shape of a bat, pronounced "fu," which also means good luck. The planting sits in a suiban (water tray) decorated with a pattern of *svastikah* (a sanskrit word that means "being fortunate"). In China, the pattern is called Wan Zi and is a symbol of immortality. The emblem also appears on Buddha, representing the Seal of the Heart of Buddha.

The two mountains represent yang, and yin is symbolized in the latticework pattern of interwoven branches, twigs, and foliage that crisscrosses the open space at the center of the planting.

setting up

Needle and thread
Use a strong sewing needle and thread to affix the fiberglass cloth to the chicken wire.

◄ Chicken wire
Wire with a ½-inch (13mm) mesh is used to create the initial shape of the rocks.

Coarse and fine pebbles ►
Pebbles are used to fill the container beneath the plantings. They should be kept damp to provide moisture to the plants.

Protective clothing
Always wear gloves and a face mask when working with fiberglass cloth and cement.

Wire cutters
You will need wire cutters to cut the chicken wire.

▼ Patterned Japanese suiban
The shallow suiban (water tray) I chose for this landscape is decorated with good luck symbols. It can hold a layer of pebbles about 1 inch (25mm) thick.

Newspaper
Wrap the ciment-fondu rock in damp newspaper while it sets.

◄ Ciment fondu
Ciment fondu provides the solid bulk of the rock.

► Brush
A brush is needed to apply the mixed ciment fondu to the fiberglass cloth. An artist's brush is ideal.

► Wire
Ordinary aluminum or copper wire, available from hardware stores, can be used for wiring the figurines to the landscape.

Constructing the landscape

Start by making a sketch of the mountains, which should have a batlike appearance, as shown. Spread a piece of plastic sheeting on your work surface. Wear protective gloves when working with the chicken wire and a face mask when mixing and applying the ciment fondu.

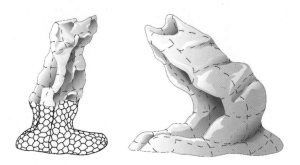

① Cut and mold chicken wire into the basic shapes of the mountain rocks, and cover the wire frame with fiberglass cloth. (See pages 12–13 for full instructions.) Attach the cloth by stitching at ½-inch (13mm) intervals with a needle and thread. In a bowl, mix up the ciment fondu according to the package instructions. Using a brush, cover the cloth with ciment fondu, and make ledges and crevices in which to plant trees and stand figurines. Wrap the rock in wet newspaper and plastic, and seal for 24 hours. After it is fully set, rinse the rock.

② When the rocks are dry, use quick-drying cement to attach them to the base of the water tray. Ciment-fondu rocks weather nicely with time when left outside. The rocks featured in this landscape have been weathered for several years. Scatter pebbles of various sizes in the water tray to create the effect of a river. Start with fine pebbles in the center of the river and graduate to coarse pebbles at the riverbank.

◀ **Raffia**
Raffia is useful for tying trees in place in the landscape while the sticky sedge peat is drying. After 12 hours, the mixture will have hardened, the trees will be secure, and the raffia can be cut away.

▶ **Figurines**
These are available at stores that sell Chinese ceramic pots for bonsai.

▶ **Sedge peat**
Use sedge peat to create planting pockets (see page 14) and as a planting medium for the landscape.

◀ **Quick-drying cement**
I use quick-drying cement to affix the rocks to the water tray.

Fiberglass cloth
Fiberglass cloth covers the chicken wire before the ciment fondu is applied.

▶ **Epoxy glue**
Use extra-strong glue to attach short lengths of wire to the base of the figurines.

▶ **Mixing bowl**
A mixing bowl will be needed to mix the ciment fondu.

Plastic sheeting
Use plastic sheeting to protect your work surface from the ciment fondu and to wrap around the newspaper covering the ciment-fondu rock while it sets.

Chick grit
Chick grit is useful as coarse drainage. It is available at farm and feed supply stores.

Planting plan

Prepare planting pockets with sedge peat at the top of each rock (see page 14) and in the ledges and crevices. In each planting area, place a thin layer of chick grit, then at the top of each rock put the elm trees with their bonsai pads. The landscape is planted in the shape of a bat with outstretched wings. The two trees should appear to have grown around the mountains, with their branches forming a lacy vista. Carefully position your trees and tie them into position with raffia.

Mix sedge peat with water to create a thick, creamy consistency and pour it over the root area of the trees. Plant the sedum and rhododendron in this wet sedge peat. Position them as marked on the diagram at right. The medium takes 12 hours to harden; after that, the trees will be secured to the rock and you can remove the raffia.

"Plant" the figurines of the immortals so they appear to have descended from the clouds. Glue wire to the bases of the figurines so they can be speared into the sedge-peat mix. Finish by adding chick grit and pebbles where needed.

1. *Ulmus parvifolia*
2. *Rhododendron intricatum*
3. *Sedum hispanicum*
4. Moss
5. Li T'ieh Kuai
6. Lu Tung Pin
7. Ts'ao Kuo Chiu
8. Ho Hsien Ku
9. Han Hsiang Tzu
10. Lan Tsai Ho
11. Chung Li Ch'uan
12. Chang Kuo Lao

CARE

- **Positioning:** Place the landscape in a bright position outdoors but out of strong sun. Keep away from strong drying winds and very intense sunlight, which will shrivel the leaves. Elms are half-hardy, so some winter protection is necessary.
- **Watering:** Elms like ample water on both their roots and their leaves. On hot days you may need to water in both the morning and evening to ensure that the soil does not dry out.
- **Feeding:** Apply a mild liquid bonsai fertilizer once a month from January to June.
- **Pruning:** Chinese elms are vigorous trees; trim the branches back so two or three leaves remain on the sides of each branch throughout the bulk of the tree. At the top, trim back to two or three leaves. Tidy up the rhododendrons by clipping them into a ball shape when necessary.

---

the scenery

▼ *Rhododendron intricatum*

The single rhododendron in the landscape grows to about 1 foot (30cm) tall. For bonsai, it is best to take cuttings, because a plant that has already developed a rootball will need too large a planting hole. Stick fresh cuttings directly into the medium of the landscape. *R. intricatum* has small lavender-blue flowers and extremely small leaves. It prefers cool conditions.

▼ *Sedum hispanicum*

I harvested the sedum for this project from a gravelly area in a seaside garden. The plant had formed clumps of woody branches, which are ideal for this landscape because this type of growth prevents soil from being washed away and adds texture to the ground surface. *S. hispanicum* is a self-propagating alpine. You will need three plants to recreate this landscape.

▶ *Ulmus parvifolia*

Chinese elm is a hardy and durable tree that is readily available from garden centers. Imported from China, it tolerates cool conditions outdoors and hot, dry conditions indoors, though it requires more maintenance indoors. When grown outside, the bark develops a lovely yellow tinge and the leaves are an attractive pink in fall. You will need two trees for this landscape. Small-leaf varieties of Chinese elm are best for bonsai.

▼ Moss

An attractive ground cover, moss is used to hide the planting medium. See page 9 for suggestions on gathering and storing moss.

Root clasped to rock

The Eight Immortals scene includes trees that appear to clasp the rock with the roots exposed. Because you make your own rock, you can make dips and crevices to help the planting stay in position. If you decide to use real rocks, you will need to use the following traditional method to create a rock-clinging bonsai.

TIP

You can make your own rock (see pages 12–13), or bonsai specialty stores supply suitable rock for this style of planting. It is often imported from Japan and has an interesting texture and color. Before planting, look at the rock from all angles and decide which is going to be the front.

1 The tree will need to have been trained to have long roots. This is achieved in a training box available from bonsai suppliers. Every 4 months or so, remove a layer of soil to expose more roots and encourage them to grow longer.

2 Remove the soil from the roots and separate them so they fall evenly over the rock. Attach lengths of wire to the rock with epoxy glue. Once the glue has dried, wire the roots to the rock and, if necessary, tie the tree in place with raffia. Then, spread a thin layer of sedge peat over the roots.

3 Wrap the entire rock and roots with sphagnum moss and tie it with raffia, then place it in a container that is deep enough to cover the base of the tree. Leave the tree to settle for approximately 6 to 8 months.

4 Once the tree has settled, remove it from the container and check to see that there is no damage to the roots from the wire. Wash the moss and sedge peat from the top of the rock to expose the roots. Over time, they will take on an aged, smooth appearance. The rock can now be placed in the suiban.

▶ Eight Immortals

Ho Hsien Ku is the daughter of a herbalist and she holds a lotus flower. She helps take care of the home and is revered by women.

Ho Hsien Ku

Chung Li Ch'uan, chief of the immortals, is an ex-general who is bare-bellied and fat. He clutches a fan, which he uses to bring souls in the underworld back to life.

Chung Li Ch'uan

Han Hsiang Tzu holds a flute. He is the patron of musicians.

Han Hsiang Tzu

Lan Tsai Ho is usually regarded as a woman, but her/his gender is not known for certain. Lan Tsai Ho holds a basket of flowers and assists florists.

Chang Kuo Lao is an old scholar, a recluse, and an advisor to the Emperors. He usually carries a bamboo musical instrument.

Lan Tsai Ho

Li T'ieh Kuai, a patron of pharmacists, appears as a lame beggar with an iron crutch. He assists physicians.

Chang Kuo Lao

Ts'ao Kuo Chiu

Ts'ao Kuo Chiu wears official robes and a cap and carries a pair of castanets. He is a renowned geomancer (mystic) and a patron of actors and historians.

Lu Tung Pin

Li T'ieh Kuai

Lu Tung Pin is a priest and scholar who carries a horsehair flyswatter and has a two-edged sword slung across his back. He is greatly revered by the sick.

八仙 Ba Xian
EIGHT IMMORTALS

CHINESE ELM
AT A GLANCE

🌿 One of the best species of tree for bonsai, *Ulmus parvifolia* is a deciduous species that has small leaves and a fine tracery of branches if pruned constantly. In very warm climates, the tree can be reluctant to drop its leaves and will remain evergreen.

🌿 The fine branches of Chinese elm can be trained into broom style (see page 45), while the roots are naturally long and flexible and lend themselves to training in various root-clasped-to-rock styles (see page 27).

🌿 Chinese elm grows wild in Japan and Korea, as well as in China. It prefers lots of light and sun and requires daily watering throughout the summer and twice daily on very hot days. Protect it from very hot sun to prevent the leaves from scorching. The roots should be protected from frost.

Shi Liu

ABUNDANCE

At the center of this graceful arrangement is a majestic pomegranate *(Punica granatum),* which is also called stone willow. The pomegranate has seeded itself on the topmost peak of a mountain and grown into a fine specimen. Over the years, harsh weather has split the base of the tree. Its triangular shape is echoed in the formation of the rock below, and the opening offers an inviting walkway to the beyond.

On the left of the landscape are two 8-year-old cuttings of the *neijikan* (Japanese for "twisted trunk") pomegranate. Their exposed roots look like dragons tumbling down the mountainside. When the seeds of the pomegranate are ripe, the pod appears to smile as it splits open, ready for the seeds to burst forth. I have always been drawn to this tree, which represents fertility; when it is given as a wedding gift, it is said to bestow an abundance of offspring upon the newlyweds. It also represents laughter and is revered as a holy tree.

The landscape rests in an Italian, hand-finished, terra-cotta water tray, which has an aesthetically pleasing shape for this particular arrangement. It is also narrow enough to sit on a windowsill, allowing you to group two or more landscapes.

setting up

◄ Rectangular terra-cotta water tray
I chose a handmade tray that was a bright terra-cotta color when new. I used ceramic paints to tone down the hue and give the pottery an aged appearance.

Needle and thread
A sewing needle and cotton thread are used to affix fiberglass cloth to chicken wire.

Mixing bowl
This is used for mixing the ciment fondu.

Wire cutters
You will need wire cutters to cut the chicken wire.

Protective clothing
Always wear a face mask when using cement and gloves when working with fiberglass cloth.

◄ Quick-drying cement
This is useful for affixing ciment-fondu rocks to the base of the tray.

Plastic sheeting
Protect your work surface from the ciment fondu with plastic sheeting. Also wrap it around the wet newspaper used to cover the ciment fondu while it sets.

Fiberglass cloth
Fiberglass cloth is available from craft and art supply stores (it is often used to make model airplanes). Sheets in various sizes and weights are available.

Newspaper
Wrap the ciment-fondu rock in damp newspaper while it sets. Wrap plastic around the newspaper to prevent it from drying out.

◄ Paintbrush
I find ciment fondu is best applied with a paintbrush ½ to 1 inch (12–25mm) wide, as the mixture can be applied quickly and thickly.

Constructing the landscape

Start by making a sketch of your finished rock. Spread a piece of plastic sheeting on your work surface. Wear protective gloves when working with the chicken wire and a face mask when mixing and applying the ciment fondu.

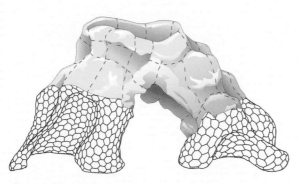

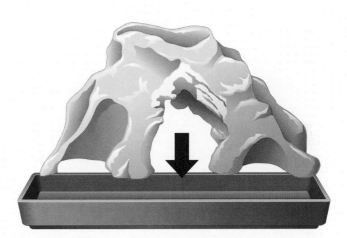

1 Following the ciment-fondu method described on pages 12–13, cut and shape the chicken wire to resemble a bridge, then cover it with fiberglass cloth and stitch it in place. The chicken wire will not need any additional support for this shape.

Make sure the rock is of the proper dimensions to fit in the water tray, then mix the ciment fondu in a bowl and work it onto the form with a paintbrush to make the surface look like weather-beaten rock. Wrap it in damp newspaper, then cover with plastic until it has set—approximately 24 hours. After it is fully set, rinse the rock.

2 Paint the tray with ceramic paint. I used dark silver gray with a metallic finish. Allow 12 hours for the paint to dry. When both the rock and the tray are dry, use quick-drying cement to attach the rock to the tray. It will set within 1 hour.

◄Sedge peat
When planting trees clasped onto rocks, use sedge peat or a sticky combination of ½ cup peat, ½ cup clay, and ¼ cup water. The mixture will help the roots stick to the rock and will harden after 12 hours or so.

►Raffia
Raffia is useful for tying trees to the rock while the roots set.

Ceramic paint
I like to paint new terra-cotta trays, as they tend to be rather bright in color. Terra-cotta fades in time, so this is not absolutely necessary.

Chicken wire
Use ½-inch (10mm) wire mesh to create the initial shape and structure of the rock.

◄Bonsai soil mix
Available from bonsai suppliers, bonsai soil mix is usually one part loam, two parts sphagnum peat moss, and two parts granite grit.

▼Pebbles
Pebbles of various colors and sizes are useful for decorating the finished landscape. They can be used to form river banks and pathways.

Ciment fondu
Available from building and masonry suppliers, ciment fondu provides the solid bulk of the rock and could also be used in place of quick-drying cement. Follow the manufacturer's instructions.

▲Florist's wire
Cut into short pieces and bent into hairpin shapes, green florist's wire is ideal for affixing moss to a landscape.

Planting plan

Use rolls of sedge peat to form planting areas (see page 14). Position the central pomegranate tree. I have placed this one slanting to the right. If it were upright at the top of the rock it would look unnatural, because in such a position in the wild it would be exposed to the wind and bend away from the mountain. Place the other two trees on the left of the rock, then pour wet sedge peat around the roots. Tie the trees in place with raffia until the liquid mix sets around their roots. One pomegranate cutting with exposed, dragonlike roots (see page 57) should be placed on the left slope. The second cutting is placed at the foot of the mountain.

The thyme is planted on the right to balance the scene; the azorella is to the left of the tree, and the pilea is underneath the thyme. The saxifrage and the geraniums are tumbling down the mountain on the left. You do not need to follow this plan, but try to use light-colored foliage to emphasize sunny areas and dark foliage to accentuate shadows. Arrange moss speared with florist's wire in places where it would grow naturally, such as the dark, damp areas. Place soil mix and pebbles around the landscape to suggest pathways and rocks.

CARE

- **Positioning:** Place the landscape in full sun for part of the day. Keep it warm in winter. I keep this planting all year in a northwest-facing greenhouse, where it receives approximately 3 hours of sunshine a day. The landscape cannot tolerate too much sun.
- **Watering:** The flat rootage of this landscape makes it important to water it regularly. Water daily with rainwater until the soil is moist and the rock is completely wet. Mist with a fine spray each evening from March to October.
- **Feeding:** Feed once a month from March to October with bonsai fertilizer.
- **Pruning:** Allow the pomegranate growth to develop; when the leaves turn dark green, prune back the branch to a new side bud. Repeat the process throughout the growing season.

---

1. *Punica granatum*
2. *Thymus vulgaris*
3. *Pilea microphylla*
4. Moss
5. *Geranium robertianum*
6. *Saxifraga cochlearis*
7. *Azorella trifurcata*

the scenery

◀ Punica granatum
When grown from cuttings, pomegranate will flower when it is only a few years old. However, trimming and pruning depletes the flower buds. It flowers on the previous year's wood, so it will take 2 to 3 years to become established. The main specimen in this landscape is about 50 years old; I have had it for nearly 25 years. It has attractive multiple trunks. There are also two cuttings of *Punica granatum* that are 6 to 8 years old.

▼ Thymus vulgaris
Thyme is a deliciously fragrant culinary herb. You can trim it frequently and use the clippings in cooking. It has fairly woody stems and light-colored foliage, which gives an illusion of sunshine in the scene. Its dense growth makes it ideal in landscape design. I used one plant in the landscape.

▼ Azorella trifurcata
This alpine has tiny, densely packed leaves, and it's often mistaken for a moss. It is a bright, luxuriant green, and I used two plants here to create an impression of dappled sunlight among the trees. The richness and soft form also offer a pleasing contrast to the wood. It tolerates root disturbance and root pruning.

▼ Pilea microphylla
This artillery plant thrives in moist conditions and must be protected from frost. Propagate from ½ inch (12mm) cuttings inserted in horticultural sand. When root growth starts, trim or pluck to the desired shape, and plant in your bonsai garden. I have used two clipped plants here.

Clump style

1 You will first need to choose a suitable tree to train in the clump style. Some trees will grow multiple trunks naturally; others can be encouraged. Choose a tree with lots of low branches. Anticipate growing the tree into three ball shapes. This will give you a good guide when looking for a suitable tree.

2 Once you have selected the new trunks, tie down the branches with wire or raffia to encourage them to grow away from the main trunk. Pull the main trunk down toward the left or right. Remove one third of the growth to induce more branches to form.

3 Trim the trunks of the branches, leaving two or three branches at the end of each one. Keep the main part of the branch bare but allow it to develop its own branches as it thickens and ages. Think of each of these trunks as individual trees and prune the branches accordingly. This will give a nice network of branches.

4 Move the tree to a flat dish to induce good branch structure. Leave some root exposed, which will exaggerate the clump style. Branches tend to echo root growth, and on flat dishes the roots grow outward. The branches mirror this and grow horizontally, rather than upward.

▶ *Saxifraga cochlearis*
This attractive alpine has dainty rosettes of delicate blue-green leaves, and looks very attractive planted along one side of the rock. Every year the clump increases in size. Prune it as needed to keep it in bounds. In most landscapes, soil drying is a problem. Alpines and mosses play an important role in moisture retention, because they act as reservoirs for excess water. You will need one plant in this landscape.

Moss
An attractive ground cover, moss is used to hide the planting medium. See page 9 for suggestions on gathering and storing moss.

▶ *Geranium robertianum*
The single herb Robert at the base of the rock is a self-seeded plant. It sprouted 3 years ago, and I did not have the heart to remove it. A wild geranium that grows prolifically in wild and waste areas, it adds a delicate contrast to the powerful rock and twisting roots. I tend to cut back its long stems and remove any large leaves. I find that using grasses, or in this case, a wild geranium, in the landscape helps the soil. The constant drying out and watering seems to prevent it from becoming waterlogged.

Shi Lui
ABUNDANCE

POMEGRANATE
AT A GLANCE

🌿 *Punica granatum* is grown for its flowers, fruit, and attractive trunk. It is a deciduous tree with twiggy branches and narrow leaves that drop in fall unless the tree is grown indoors. In midsummer, red flowers form at the end of new shoots.

🌿 Pomegranate bark is pale and contrasts well with the foliage. The trunk tends to grow in a twisted fashion and lends itself to many bonsai styles.

🌿 This tree is native to Asia and Mediterranean regions and thrives best in warm climates. In temperate climates, it may not produce fruit. It should be kept outdoors in summer. In northern climates, it needs protection from cold in winter.

公雞山

Gong Ji Shan
ROOSTER MOUNTAIN

With its head held high, as if defying the heavens, Rooster Mountain dominates this landscape like a rooster crowing at heaven's door. In feng shui, the rooster represents new beginnings and happenings—it is an animal of the future and is also believed to ward off evil spirits.

An aged octopus-style juniper (*Juniperus procumbens* 'Nana') leans toward the mountain. A group of raft-style junipers (*Juniperus chinensis*) adds further perspective and depth. At the front of the landscape, a boatman waits to take you on a meandering voyage up the river toward a pair of sunlit lemon thyme *(Thymus* x *citriodorus)* plants in the distance.

The rock in this landscape is a piece of natural Ying River rock from China, and the whole scene is set on a curved pottery tray. Its irregular shape adds to the flowing lines created by the river in the tableau. You can make a similar shape with ciment fondu. Round gravel in several sizes adds depth to the ground surface and has a gentle glow. Chipped pebbles reflect light and are shinier; if you prefer this effect, use them instead of round gravel. In this planting, I also used the gravel as mulch at the base of the alpine plants to keep their stems dry and prevent the soil mix from being washed away.

setting up

▲ Chick grit
Chick grit is a useful substitute for horticultural grit. It is finer and provides good drainage in a bonsai landscape. It is available at farm and feed supply stores.

▼ Sedge peat
This is an ideal planting medium for bonsai landscapes. Adding extra water makes it more liquid so that it can be poured around tree roots. It drains and solidifies in 12 to 24 hours.

Ceramic water tray
I commissioned a ceramic tray specially for this scene. Sometimes when you have a specific landscape in mind, it is easier to ask a potter to create a tray in the ideal dimensions.

Cake spatula
A flexible spatula is ideal for transferring cement or peat onto the landscapes.

► Pliers
Pliers or wire cutters are needed to cut the bonsai wire.

▼ Quick-drying cement
Used for affixing the rock to the dish, quick-drying cement usually dries within 1 hour. You should wear a face mask when working with cement.

Constructing the landscape

Start by making a sketch of your landscape. Spread a piece of plastic sheeting on your work surface. Wear a face mask when working with cement.

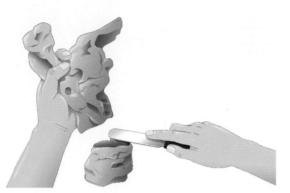

1 Carefully select pieces of Ying River rock and apply the quick-drying cement with a cake spatula to fasten them together in the shape and size of the finished mountain.

2 Allow the cement to dry for 24 hours, then attach more pieces of rock to provide height and create Rooster Mountain. After it is fully set, rinse the rock. Allow it to dry again before attaching the rocks to the water tray, again using quick-drying cement. Take care to balance the landscape visually.

◀Ying River rock
Ying River rock and other suitable rock is usually available from bonsai importers.

◀Sphagnum moss
Chopped sphagnum moss is available from garden centers. It is a highly water-retentive planting medium.

Plastic sheeting
Plastic sheeting will be necessary to protect your work surface from quick-drying cement.

▶Round gravel in various sizes or chipped pebbles
I used round gravel in this scene because it tends to absorb light and give a soft appearance. Chipped pebbles reflect light but are equally suitable.

▶Bonsai wire
Copper-colored aluminum wire is available from bonsai suppliers. It is used for securing roots to the tray and for wiring branches.

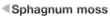

▼Bonsai soil mix
Available from specialty bonsai suppliers, this soil mix is one part loam, two parts sphagnum peat moss, and two parts granite grit.

Planting plan

Use rolls of sedge peat to form your main planting areas (see page 14). Use chick grit to form a drainage layer at the base of each planting area. Place the main octopus-style juniper against Rooster Mountain; position the tree to echo the shape of the rock. Slightly tilt the tree toward you to increase perspective. Plant the raft-style (see page 51) 'Shimpaku' juniper slightly behind the main tree, then position each of the trunks, angling the smallest tree in the group toward you. To hold the trees in place, secure them with bonsai wire. Pour wet sedge peat around the base of the trees. This will harden in 12 hours, then you can remove the wire.

Plant the honeysuckle around Rooster Mountain. Continue the line with the thyme behind the main juniper. Plant the sedum toward the front. Cover the planting area with chopped sphagnum moss to keep the soil moist, and use the round gravel and soil mix to add dry areas to the landscape. For the finishing touch, place a boat or a fishing raft to add life to the scene.

CARE

- **Positioning:** In spring, place the landscape where the morning sun can reach it. In summer, protect it from the scorching rays of the sun by moving the container to light shade.
- **Watering:** Water generously; spray foliage in the evenings during hot spells.
- **Feeding:** Feed once a month from March to October with nitrogen-rich fertilizer.
- **Pruning:** Prune the lower branches and foliage as needed to allow air to circulate. Cut only to the previous year's woody growth to avoid stimulating new growth. Pinch back any needles that become too long and spoil the shape of the tree.

1. *Thymus x citriodorus*
2. *Juniperus procumbens* 'Nana'
3. *Juniperus chinensis* 'Shimpaku'
4. Boat
5. *Sedum album* 'Coral Carpet'
6. *Lonicera nitida* 'Baggesen's Gold'

the scenery

▼ *Juniperus procumbens* 'Nana'
I grew this octopus-style juniper specimen from cuttings taken the previous spring. It is a conifer that easily develops foliage pads (see page 69). This conifer tolerates dry conditions, so it's a suitable choice for rock plantings. The 'Nana' variety tends to have much smaller needles than those of other junipers. From a distance, the foliage looks beautifully dense, which helps create a convincing scene. You will need one *J. procumbens* 'Nana' for the landscape.

▼ *Juniperus chinensis* 'Shimpaku'
This elegant juniper is a classic tree for bonsai. With its fine, blue-green needles and reddish trunk, it is an attractive conifer for landscape plantings. Wiring conifers to control their growth works well for bonsai. In this landscape, I trained this variety of juniper in the raft style (see page 51) so that it appears as a group of trees.

▼ *Lonicera nitida* 'Baggesen's Gold'
This delicate, gold-colored boxleaf honeysuckle has small leaves. It's easy to grow: stems of this shrub root almost as soon as they touch the ground. Mainly used for hedging, this plant takes well to pruning. You can clip it to almost any shape and it will bounce back, rewarding you with new, golden growth.

In this landscape, I felt the rock needed softening at the edge of the scene, so I planted three honeysuckle plants on the left. This immediately gave the montage a middle ground, creating another dimension. *L. nitida* also links the thyme and junipers to complete the scene. The foliage seemed a little too dense for the effect I wanted to achieve, so I pruned the honeysuckle to reveal some of its fine branches.

Octopus style

This style is an exaggerated form of the informal upright style, with excessive twists, turns, and curves in the branches, trunk, and often the roots. The overall effect is of a tortuous, distorted tree.

1 ▶ Junipers are ideal for this style. Choose a cutting that is 1 to 2 years old and work on it in a 1-inch (2.5cm) diameter plastic plant pot. Before wiring, choose which side will be the front of the tree, then prune out any excess foliage.

2 Begin by wiring the trunk. To get the sinuous curving trunk, bend the tree into a "C" shape and tie the top to the bottom with raffia.

3 When the branches grow long enough, bend them into "S" shapes and wire them downward to simulate an aged tree. Wiring the branches into "S" bends shortens them without cutting them and produces branches that are rich in growth, ideal for creating foliage pads.

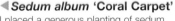

4 When the tree is wired, remove it from its old pot and comb out the roots. Prune them and replant the juniper in a shallow pot where it can begin to develop a bonsai pad. The tree should also be pruned to form foliage pads (see page 69).

5 After approximately 12 months, the wired branches will be trained into shape and the wire can be removed. New branches should be wired in the same way. Because this technique is started on such a young cutting, it can take 10 to 12 years for a tree to look fully styled.

▼ *Thymus x citriodorus*

A culinary herb that appears to trap sunlight with its golden color, lemon thyme helps create depth in a planting. I felt the scene would benefit from a little color in the background because the junipers are mainly green and brown, and this variety of thyme does the job nicely. It is like a spiritual light in the distance, beckoning you toward it and creating a link between Rooster Mountain and the junipers. I used two plants in this scene. Trim the thyme to keep it compact.

◀ *Sedum album* 'Coral Carpet'

I placed a generous planting of sedum immediately behind the fisherman to draw attention first to the foreground and then to the naturally eroded surface of the rock. Planting it at the base of the rock covers the bank of soil immediately below it. This gives the illusion that the rock is protruding from the ground rather than simply lying on top of it. This alpine plant has rich, green-purple foliage and fleshy leaves that echo the shape of the gravel. As the plant becomes older, the leaves take on a reddish color, which adds contrast. Use four plants in your landscape.

▼ Boatman

This figurine directs your gaze to the foreground and then leads you into the scenery. The figure reminds me of the boatmen of Kweilin, China, who row down the Likiang River in the late afternoon, usually with cormorants perched beside them on the boat. At night time the fishing begins, and the birds have a ring fitted around their necks so they can't swallow the fish they catch.

Gong Ji Shan

ROOSTER MOUNTAIN

JUNIPER
AT A GLANCE

❧ Widely distributed throughout the world, juniper (*Juniperus* spp.) lend themselves to all bonsai styles, except for broom style. They are relatively hardy and long-lived, and the bark takes on an aged appearance while relatively young.

❧ These trees have two types of foliage. Some only have what is called "juvenile" foliage, which is needlelike, some have scalelike adult foliage, and others have a mixture of both. Bonsai growers prefer to choose a variety with only one type of growth. Foliage color ranges from blue-green to light green. Pinch out new foliage throughout the year.

❧ Juniper's natural living conditions are heathland and desert, so they prefer dry conditions and full sun. The foliage can scorch in very hot sun, so some shade should be provided. Water daily in summer, but in winter just keep the soil moist.

Li Bai
THE DREAMING POET

According to legend, Li Bai—a poet of the Tang Dynasty—once dreamed that the tip of his writing brush had burst into bloom. This is an inspiring legend to interpret using bonsai. I chose to depict the blooming paintbrush as a trumpetlike ciment-fondu rock, with a burst of foliage provided by a juniper (*Juniperus procumbens* 'Nana'). For this landscape, I used three separate trays for planting. The number three is important in Chinese philosophy—the triad represents heaven, Earth, and humankind.

When creating a landscape, a garden master selects stones to express the powerful upward thrust of a wave. For the mountain in this landscape, I formed a handmade rock into the shape of a rising wave that is just at the point of breaking. The plantings and grasses at the top of the mountain resemble the foam at the crest of the wave.

The larger tray depicts power and movement, whereas the two smaller trays, with their delicate plantings, are set apart and peaceful. When you look at the landscape as a whole, you can sense the stillness of space and catch the fresh scent of the trees carried in the breeze. The spontaneous natural forms of the three plantings almost appear to create a cosmic dance.

setting up

◄ Three circular terra-cotta trays
These should measure approximately 14 inches (35cm), 12 inches (30cm), and 10 inches (25cm) in diameter.

Dark brown terra-cotta paint
You can use terra-cotta paint to color the trays a warm, dark brown and blend them into the landscape.

Ericaceous soil mix
This soil mix is essential for acid-loving plants, such as rhododendron.

▼ Chicken wire
Build the tall rock in the landscape out of chicken wire.

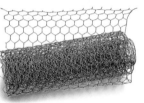

Newspaper
This is used to cover ciment-fondu rock for 24 hours until dry (see page 13).

Needle and thread
Any needle and thread is suitable for sewing the fiberglass cloth to the chicken wire.

▼ Paintbrush
Ciment fondu can be applied with any brush. I find one that is about ½ to 1 inch (12–25mm) wide most suitable, as it means the mixture can be applied quickly and thickly.

◄ Mixing bowl
A mixing bowl will be necessary for holding the ciment-fondu mixture.

Cake spatula
A flexible spatula is ideal for transferring cement or peat onto the landscapes.

► Ciment fondu
Available from building and masonry suppliers, ciment fondu is a light form of cement. It takes up to 24 hours to dry.

Constructing the landscape

Wash and dry the three circular trays and apply two coats of terra-cotta paint to each tray. Let dry. Spread a piece of plastic sheeting on your work surface. Wear protective gloves when working with the chicken wire and a face mask when mixing and applying the ciment fondu.

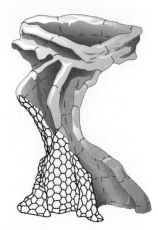

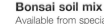 Cut the chicken wire to size and stitch the fiberglass cloth onto it as tightly as possible—the tighter the stitch, the finer the result will be. Try to aim for a wafer-thin appearance. (See pages 12–13 for a full explanation of creating a ciment-fondu rock.) Flare out the base of the rock so that it will be stable. Create bends and curves in the remainder of the wire and cloth to replicate the strong, wavelike lines of the rock.

❷ Remember to make a cavity in the top of the rock for the juniper planting, as well as in the other planting areas. In a bowl, mix up the ciment fondu according to the package instructions. With a paintbrush, apply it to the molding, making the covering look natural. Paint it on thinly to cover, then sprinkle it with chick grit for texture. Cover with damp newspaper and plastic. Allow the fondu to set for 24 hours. After it is fully set, rinse the rock. Use a cake spatula to apply quick-drying cement, and attach the rock to the large tray.

▶ Chick grit
Use chick grit as an alternative to horticultural grit. It is available at farm and feed supply stores.

Plastic sheeting
Protect your work surface with plastic sheeting. Also use it to wrap the ciment-fondu rock when it is covered in wet newspaper.

Bonsai soil mix
Available from specialty bonsai suppliers, this soil mix is one part loam, two parts sphagnum peat moss, and two parts granite grit.

Fiberglass cloth
Small sheets of fiberglass, readily available from craft and art supply stores, are layered on the chicken wire frame to create a nonporous base to which the ciment fondu is applied. This three-layer structure gives the optimum combination of strength and light weight.

▼ Protective clothing
Always wear a face mask when working with cement and gloves when handling fiberglass cloth.

▶ Wire cutters
These are needed to cut the chicken wire.

▶ Florist's wire
Pins made from short lengths of florist's wire bent into a "U" shape are ideal for pinning moss in place.

Sedge peat
This is an ideal planting medium for the bonsai landscapes.

Quick-drying cement
Useful for affixing the ciment-fondu rocks to the base of the tray, this cement dries in approximately 1 hour.

Planting plan

Place chick grit in the base of the planting cavity at the top of the rock, position the juniper, then pour in bonsai soil mixture around the roots. Use sedge peat around the edges, if necessary, to secure the tree in position. Position the heathers, the sedum, and the 'Frosted Curls' around the base of the juniper, and cover the exposed mix with moss. Dust any areas not covered with moss with chick grit to help retain moisture. At the base of the rock, add ericaceous soil mix and set the sedge in place on the left. Arrange the cotoneaster plants so they tumble over one another. I have placed the two *Cotoneaster congestus* at the front and the *C. conspicuus* at the back. Build up the soil layer with sedge peat and scatter some silver-coated pebbles between the plants.

In the medium-sized tray, place the maple at an attractive angle and plant the two cypress spurges beside it. The maple's bonsai pad will fill most of the tray. Fill empty areas with bonsai soil mix. Arrange the moss to cover exposed soil and use florist's wire pins to secure it in place so that it won't be washed away during watering. In the small tray, plant the rhododendron using ericaceous soil mix and attach moss to exposed areas as before.

Position your landscape. Notice how the sizes and heights of the plantings play an important part in the scene's perspective.

CARE

- **Positioning:** Only the maple needs at least 3 hours of sun per day. Keep the large and small trays in a sheltered spot outdoors.
- **Watering:** Check the trays daily. Do not allow them to dry out.
- **Feeding:** Supply each tray with a pellet of organic bonsai fertilizer once a month.
- **Pruning:** When the juniper starts to lose its shape or look untidy, pinch the growing tips with your fingertips. Avoid using your nails, which can cause browning on the pinched ends.

1. *Juniper procumbens* 'Nana'
2. *Carex comans* 'Frosted Curls'
3. Moss
4. *Erica carnea* 'December Red'
5. *Sedum hispanicum*
6. *Cotoneaster congestus*
7. *C. conspicuus*
8. *Rhododendron impeditum*
9. *Euphorbia cyparissias*
10. *Acer palmatum* 'Shindeshojo'

the scenery

▼*Juniperus procumbens* 'Nana'

With time, the mature growth of a Japanese garden juniper (*J. procumbens*) will create the undulating lines of the 12-year-old tree shown in the main photo. However, a 3-year-old tree, such as this one, also looks very attractive planted on the mountaintop so that it appears to tumble over the edge of the precipice. You need one plant for this landscape.

▼*Acer palmatum* 'Shindeshojo'

The Japanese red maple in the landscape is 12 years old. Maples are one of the most popular species for bonsai because of their beautiful coloring, delicate shape, and fine leaves.

Moss

I obtained this moss from a garage roof. See page 9 for suggestions on gathering and storing moss.

▼*Carex comans* 'Frosted Curls'

This plant provides contrast to the solid structure of the rock and the rounded forms of the cotoneaster and juniper in the larger tray. Its linear growth also adds movement to the scenery. 'Frosted Curls' can grow quite large. Over time, you may need to pull out this plant and replace it if it outgrows the landscape. One plant is needed here.

▶*Sedum hispanicum*

I used this because of its attractive grapelike leaves, which hang beautifully over the edge of the rocklike vine. A single plant adds movement to the scene, and the color contrasts nicely with the green of the juniper.

Erica carnea 'December Red'

There are many different varieties of heather. The two small heathers used here have purple flowers and provide visual balance for the juniper.

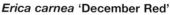

Broom style

The rhododendron in the Li Bai landscape has been pruned in the broom style. Traditionally, broom style is applied to upright deciduous trees, and the effect aimed for is that of an upturned Japanese broom. The style can be used on many types of trees, especially deciduous ones, which reveal the delicate tracery of branches after the leaves fall. Rhododendrons also lend themselves to this style.

TIP
Depending on the style of your landscape, you can vary the amount by which you reduce the branches and roots in step 4. Here, the roots have been reduced by one third so that the branches will spread close to the soil. However much you decide to cut, the branches and roots should be reduced in equal proportion.

1 Select a rhododendron that is 3 or more years old and has a thick trunk. Cut off all the foliage horizontally, 2 to 3 inches (5–7.5cm) above the base.

2 Cut a V-shaped notch at the top of the trunk, with one side just slightly higher than the other, then bind the two sides together with raffia. Like a pollarded tree, branches will grow from these two sides.

3 Allow the rhododendron to grow for a year, then bunch all the branches into your hand and cut horizontally. This cut will induce a dome shape. In spring, reduce the roots by one third.

4 Continue the process with new growth until the broom style is achieved. A pleasing broom-style rhododendron can be produced by this method in 5 or 6 years.

▼ Cotoneaster congestus
You can plant two cotoneasters as cuttings directly into the landscape. Small, 1-inch (2.5cm) cuttings grow easily on the rock—the warmth from the rocks and the sedge peat make an ideal growing medium. You need young, soft growth, so take the cuttings just above a leaf internode; they will root within 8 weeks. C. congestus flowers and fruits easily. The red berries create an illusion of a miniature apple orchard.

▼ Silver-coated pebbles
Scatter silver-coated pebbles around the base of the rock in the largest tray to break up the planting and reflect light.

Rhododendron impeditum
I chose this particular type of rhododendron because it has small leaves and linear, thin trunks. The rhododendron used in the landscape is 10 years old. You need one plant for this project.

▼ Cotoneaster conspicuus
Wintergreen cotoneaster (C. conspicuus) readily self-sows and grows well from cuttings. Its trunk thickens fairly quickly, creating a sturdy and attractive shrub. It sports a mass of white blossoms in spring, followed in late summer and fall by lovely orange berries. I put one at the base of the mountain and, through constant trimming, shaped cloudlike pads of foliage to represent steps to heaven. Allow wintergreen cotoneaster to grow for 6 years to reach the right size for planting in the landscape.

▼ Euphorbia cyparissias
Cypress spurge (E. cyparissias) has fine, copper-tinged foliage with lime-green flowers in spring. It requires well-drained, moist soil. In the landscape, the two plants contrast with the texture and color of the Japanese red maple.

Li Bai

THE DREAMING POET

COTONEASTER
AT A GLANCE

❧ Cotoneaster is a popular shrub that is ideal for bonsai training in many styles, including informal upright and clasped to rock. Most species are prostrate shrubs, but some will grow into trees, such as *Cotoneaster frigidus*. Some varieties are deciduous; others are evergreen. *C. horizontalis* is perhaps the most popular variety for bonsai.

❧ This plant has small leaves, white or pink flowers, and red- to coral-colored fruit. It is an ideal beginner's plant because it is easy to grow and tolerant of most light and soil conditions.

❧ Although it can be kept indoors, cotoneaster is more successfully grown outdoors. It is fairly hardy but should be protected from frost.

Feng Hong
RED WIND—THE PHOENIX

This landscape captures the moods of the changing seasons and the elements of thunder, lightning, wind, and rain. It features a group of Japanese maples (*Acer palmatum* 'Shindeshojo')—formed from a raft-style tree (see page 51)—on one side of a path, with a single maple on the other. The red foliage contrasts with the green moss. These two colors are symbolic in Chinese painting: green for spring, red for the life force.

In spring, the maples burst into a flush of rose-pink leaves. This vibrant color symbolizes the most auspicious creature in feng shui—the red phoenix, a creature that offers the promise of hope and joy. The maples represent the phoenix extending its wings into the wind, for a split second turning the atmosphere red, hence the name Feng Hong, "red wind." The phoenix embodies the deity Feng Bo, also known as Feng Shen, who is associated with the color red and is the god and goddess of thunder, lightning, wind, and rain.

The landscape sits in a handmade, irregularly shaped, unglazed tray that adds to the natural effect of the scene. The gravel pathway draws the viewer into the landscape and toward infinity. I have worked on this landscape for more than 20 years, and it is now in a private collection.

setting up

Tray
I chose a handmade tray, which was a bright terra-cotta color when new.

◀**Silicone glue**
This glue can be found at art and aquarium-supply stores. It is used for attaching bonsai wire to the tray.

▶**Watercolors**
I used watercolor paints to tone down the hue and give the pottery an aged appearance.

◀**Paintbrush**
You do not need to be particularly careful when applying the paint, so a thick artist's brush is ideal.

▼**Sedge peat**
This is a rich, sticky soil, ideal for affixing bonsai trees to a rocky landscape. Alternatively, you can use a 50:50 mix of peat and clay.

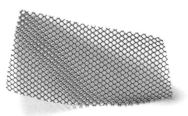

▲**Drainage mesh**
Available from bonsai suppliers and hardware stores, this mesh is placed over the drainage holes to prevent them from clogging.

Constructing the landscape

To achieve a professional look, it's best to commission an experienced potter to make the tray for this landscape. The tray must have drainage holes in the base and be irregularly shaped to represent a flat slab of rock. The tray used in this scene is approximately 24 inches (50cm) long and 12 inches (25cm) wide.

1 A newly made tray will look very clean and fresh. Paint it to create a weathered effect. Chinese watercolors are suitable; make sure you let them dry completely. Build up a wall of sedge peat around the edges. This will ensure that water does not drain away too quickly.

2 Glue lengths of bonsai wire 8 inches (20cm) long to the base of the tray in the areas you have chosen for planting. The wire will be used to secure the trees. If the trees have well-established bonsai pads, they will be freestanding and will not need to be secured with wire. Place drainage mesh over the drainage holes to prevent them from clogging with grit and soil.

▶ Akadama

Akadama is a general-purpose soil imported from Japan. It contains clay granules, which give it water-retentive properties. It can be sifted with sieves into coarse, medium, and fine grades.

▼ Coarse gravel

Coarse gravel is useful for drainage and to create pathways in the landscape.

▲ Bonsai wire

Copper-colored aluminum wire is available from bonsai suppliers. It is used to secure roots to the tray and for wiring branches.

◀ Bonsai soil mix

Available from specialty bonsai suppliers, this soil mix is one part loam, two parts spaghnum peat moss, and two parts granite grit.

▼ Chopsticks or a thin stick

Chopsticks are the perfect implement for working soil between the roots of plants.

Planting plan

If possible, choose trees that are freestanding (see page 14). Place a single maple tree on the left of the planting and a raft-style maple tree (see page 51) on the right. Once you have planned the arrangement, remove the trees, then surround each planting area with sticky sedge peat to form a wall. This will prevent the soil from washing away when the plant is watered. Put a layer of coarse akadama in the base of each planting area to act as drainage. Place the group planting in position on the tray along with its bonsai pad and secure it in position with wire, if necessary. Add a little more coarse akadama around the roots for drainage. Combine one part bonsai soil mix and one part medium akadama and work this mixture between the roots using a chopstick. Finally, add a layer of fine akadama. Repeat the process with the single maple on the left.

Plant clumps of moss to cover any exposed soil. Use the coarse gravel to create a gently curving path between the single tree and the raft-style tree. Make the path wider at the front of the scene, gradually becoming narrower as it extends to the back.

1. *Acer palmatum* 'Shindeshojo'
2. *Acer palmatum* 'Shindeshojo'—raft style
3. Moss

CARE

- **Positioning:** Place the landscape outdoors, protected from strong wind and sun. Provide at least 2 to 3 hours of sun a day to maintain the red foliage; keep in dappled shade when the sun is very hot.
- **Watering:** Water once a day in spring and summer, twice a day during hot spells. In fall, water once a day or less if the weather is cool.
- **Feeding:** Feed with pellets of organic bonsai fertilizer once a month until late summer.
- **Pruning:** Allow new shoots to develop three to five leaves, then trim each shoot back to one or two leaves. At the top of the tree, trim shoots back to two leaves.

the scenery

▶Japanese maple cuttings

These cuttings (right) were taken in the summer when the leaves were just beginning to turn green. They are now about 2 years old. To root a maple cutting, cut off a 2-inch (5cm) shoot immediately above a leaf node and dip the base of the cutting into rooting powder. Fill a small pot with soil mix and push approximately 1 inch (2.5cm) of the cutting into the soil. Cover the cutting and the pot with a plastic bag and keep in an unheated greenhouse or coldframe; make sure the bag does not touch the leaves. Roots should form within 8 weeks.

▶Raft-style 'Shindeshojo'

This group of Japanese maples is created using the raft style (see above). The group is composed of several branches from one trunk, trained to appear as a group of trees.

Both the raft-style tree and the single tree will need to develop a good pad of fibrous roots, known as a bonsai pad (see page 14) before you can plant them in the landscape. With their roots formed into a pad, the trees should be freestanding.

Raft style

Raft style gives the appearance of several trees growing together in a group but, in fact, all the trees grow from a single trunk. Raft-style trees look particularly impressive "running" down mountain slopes.

❶ ▶ Raft-style bonsai can be achieved with most tree species, but it is easier to select one that has fairly pliable branches, such as yew, pine, or Japanese maple. You could also try trees that produce suckers from exposed roots, such as elm. When selecting a specimen to train, pick a tree with a fairly long, straight trunk, then prune the tree and remove the branches from one side.

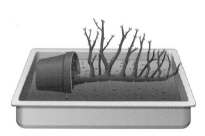

❷ Lay the tree on its side in a seed tray on a layer of bonsai soil mix, with the uncut branches pointing upward. Cut the underside of the trunk at 1-inch (2.5cm) intervals, and peel back the cambium. This will speed new root growth. Brush with rooting hormone and insert small pebbles to hold open the slits.

❸ Remove the pot from the base of the tree and tie in the existing roots by wrapping wires around them and the box. Top up the box with bonsai soil mix to 2 inches (5cm) above the trunk. Wire the branches—thick trees should be toward the front and smaller ones further back to create a sense of perspective.

❹ Once the tree has started to take root, cut out selected branches to create interesting distances between the trees. The bonsai pad will take 1 or 2 years to form. Once it is established, the old root system can be removed.

❺ Train each of the trees into a triangle shape in the same way as you would train an individual tree. It can take a further 2 to 3 years for a raft-style tree to take on the appearance of several trees. The raft-style maple in the Feng Hong landscape is more than 40 years old.

▼ Moss

I collect moss from old brick walls and bridges, where it forms lovely flat tufts that look dry but turn a beautiful shade of green when soaked with water. You can also scrape moss off paving stones. Lay the moss on dry newspaper and cover it with more newspaper. Store it this way in an airtight container until you need it for a landscape (see page 9).

▶ *Acer palmatum* 'Shindeshojo'

Shindeshojo is Japanese for "new red," and the red of this cultivar is perfect for the Feng Hong landscape. If you cannot locate 'Shindeshojo', *A. palmatum* 'Bloodgood' will work well. I have also tried *A. palmatum* 'Seigen', which has finer leaves, but I found that the leaves were highly susceptible to disease, windburn, and sunscald. 'Shindeshojo' is more resilient, though its growth habit is more upright than that of 'Seigen'. This influences the training of the tree; I use a clip-and-grow method (see page 75) to train 'Shindeshojo'.

TIPS

• Clip (prune) the planting very tightly to the desired shape, then allow new branches to form. When the first flush of leaves appears, allow each shoot to produce four or five well-developed leaves. Then cut each shoot back to two leaves. Allow the tree to grow throughout the remainder of the season, then trim it to shape after the leaves have fallen or early the following spring.

• In its natural surroundings, Japanese maple spends most of its life under the canopy of other trees, fed by a constant mist. To mimic those conditions, choose a protected spot for your landscape where it won't receive too much sun.

風
紅

Feng Hong
RED WIND—THE PHOENIX

Ping Guo
PEACE

In China, the apple—Ping Guo—signifies peace, and I designed this landscape to reflect its stillness and beauty. A 50-year-old Chinese crab apple tree *(Malus toringoides)* appears to tumble over a rock cliff, and its exposed, gnarled roots give the tree an ancient appearance. In spring, the pure white blossoms—representing female beauty—are a welcome sight, and in fall, rose-colored fruits appear.

The tree in this landscape was grown from a seed collected at Kew Gardens in England. It was passed on to me when it was 25 years old and I have had it for 25 years, during which time I shaped it into a semicascade (see page 111). I chose a handmade pottery container to represent the mountainside, as I think it perfectly complements the beautiful blossoms and fruits. I decided to extend the landscape by planting a group of 'Golden Hornet' crab apples *(M. x zumi)*. Their delicate pink buds and pinkish white flowers on upright branches provide a stunning contrast to the tumbling shape of the white-flowered crab apple, and they create a sense of movement and perspective. The two crab apple plantings are in separate containers placed in a suiban, or water tray. Thrift *(Armeria* spp.) acts as a focal point; its grasslike appearance leads the eye to the center of the semicascade crab apple, then to the group of crab apples on the left.

setting up

▼Large suiban (water tray)
The water tray will need to be large enough to accommodate two dishes. For a large landscape, it is sometimes simpler to commission a potter to make you a tray in the size required.

◀Weatherworn rock
I used a piece of natural sandstone rock to prop up the shallow dish.

▶Bonsai soil mix
This is a ready-made soil medium of one part loam, two parts sphagnum peat moss, and two parts granite grit.

▲Half-crescent pot
This half-crescent pot, made by a specialist potter, is perfect for growing cascade trees. The extra weight of the base stabilizes the tree, and the height allows the cascade to hang unhindered.

Constructing the landscape

This landscape consists of two pots in a suiban. The pot on the left is a handmade shallow dish made from clay, while the half-crescent shaped pot on the right was bought from a specialist potter.

1 The pot shown above is an irregular-shaped shallow dish in which a group of 'Golden Hornet' crab apples is planted. I commissioned a potter to make it for me because I wanted the appearance of rocklike edges to add to the character of the landscape. There are drainage holes in the bottom of the dish.

2 The half-crescent pot stands on the right of the scene. I placed chick grit in the bottom to act as drainage and then used bonsai soil mix to build up the level. The bonsai pad of the crab apple tree was placed in the pot so that the tree hangs over the pot with its roots exposed.

3 Once planted, the shallow dish was propped up in the suiban with a weatherworn rock, but the half-crescent pot can stand alone. Water is poured into the suiban for aesthetic reasons and to give humidity to the landscape.

▶Chick grit

Chick grit is a useful substitute for horticultural grit. It is finer and provides good drainage in a bonsai landscape.

◀Sedge peat

This is an ideal planting medium for bonsai landscapes. When water is added to sedge peat, it becomes sticky and can be used to create planting pockets and bonsai pads (see page 14).

▶Akadama

This is a general-purpose soil imported from Japan. It contains clay granules, which give it water-retentive properties. Sift it at home into fine, medium, and coarse granules (see page 9).

Shallow dish

The dish used here was made from a rolled-out piece of clay that warped during firing to produce an attractive curve. You could buy a similar ceramic dish from a bonsai supplier, commission a potter to make one for you, or use a piece of slate instead.

Planting plan

Scatter coarse akadama in the shallow dish, then arrange the crab apple group on the left, using a 50:50 mix of medium akadama and bonsai soil mix in a wall of sedge peat (see page 14). Dust with fine akadama.

Create planting pockets with sedge peat above the root mass of the cascade crab apple, and plant the 'Nifty Thrifty'. The thrift will prevent the soil from washing away. Make planting pockets for the sedum and other thrifts to create the impression of a slope toward the foreground. Plant the wood violet in the foreground to draw the viewer's eye down to the water in the suiban below.

Position the two crab apple plantings in the suiban so they balance the landscape. Add moss around each planting to finish off the landscape, and cover any exposed soil mix. Dust areas beneath the trees with chick grit to give a dry appearance. In nature, greenery does not grow easily in dry, shaded areas.

1. *Malus* x *zumi* 'Golden Hornet'
2. *Malus toringoides*
3. *Armeria juniperifolia* 'Bevan's Variety'
4. *Viola sylvestris*
5. *Armeria maritima* 'Alba'
6. *Armeria maritima* 'Nifty Thrifty'
7. *Sedum hispanicum*
8. Moss

CARE

- **Positioning:** Crab apple requires 2 or 3 hours of full sun a day and plenty of air circulation in order to remain healthy.
- **Watering:** Water the planting twice a day in spring and summer. You may need to water once a day in fall and winter. Check the dish daily. Refresh the water occasionally.
- **Feeding:** Do not feed the trees while they're in flower. When the fruits have developed to half their full size, usually in late June, feed them with pellets of organic bonsai fertilizer until late fall.
- **Pruning:** In fall, trim the older branches once you can distinguish the flower buds from the leaf buds (the flower buds are furry and larger than the leaf buds). Allow 2 inches (5cm) of new growth, then select the direction in which you would like the branch to continue to grow and cut off new buds that are sprouting in other directions.

---

the scenery

Malus toringoides
The curving lines of the semicascade crab apple *(M. toringoides)* tree echo the shape of the container. You can substitute any type of crab apple in this landscape. *Malus* grows best outdoors, as it needs lots of fresh air as well as full sun. See page 111 for how to train a tree in the semicascade style. I used a single tree here.

▶*Malus* x *zumi* 'Golden Hornet'
'Golden Hornet' crab apple *(M. x zumi)* bears pinkish, roselike flowers in spring and yellow fruits in fall, and it looks delightful at both times of year. This group planting consists of eight trees grown in a group and sharing one bonsai pad (see page 63).

▶*Armeria maritima* 'Nifty Thrifty'
Thrifts *(Armeria* spp.) are seaside alpines that tolerate strong winds and salty air. 'Nifty Thrifty' has variegated, straplike foliage, and produces striking, cherry-pink flowers. You may want to cut the blossoms to avoid throwing off the balance of the landscape, or you can leave them and enjoy their bold color (they bloom only for a short period). If you cannot find 'Nifty Thrifty,' any compact variety of thrift can be used. You will need three plants here.

Armeria maritima 'Alba'
I used this plant to enhance the ground cover and give texture and light to the landscape. It has narrow, dark green leaves and small white flowers in spring and summer. A single plant is needed in this landscape.

Exposed-root style

The crab apple in the Ping Guo landscape is trained in the cascade style with exposed roots. The exposed roots not only add drama and naturalistic character to the tree but also balance the trunk. Both upright and cascade trees can have exposed roots. For training in the semicascade style, see page 111.

① ▶ The roots of this crab apple were exposed at the same time as it was being trained in the semicascade style. I started training the tree when it was 3 years old. I pruned away one third of the root system and planted the tree in a shallow tray so the bonsai pad would start to form.

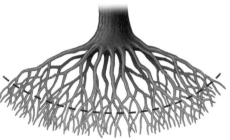

② After a year, the tree has started to form a healthy root system. Take it out of the pot, and brush away 2 inches (5cm) of soil so the roots are exposed.

③ Place bonsai soil mix in the base of the pot, higher at one side than the other, and replant the tree, this time at an angle with the roots exposed above the soil. If you are not growing your tree in semicascade style, you would simply plant the tree again on level soil with the roots exposed.

④ After 1 to 2 years of growth, remove the top inch of soil. The exposed roots will thicken and take on a gnarled appearance. Repeat this process until enough root is exposed for the tree to be aesthetically pleasing.

⑤ While the tree is being trained to have exposed roots it will also be forming a good bonsai pad (see page 14). When the pad is fully formed, the tree is ready to be transferred into the landscape.

▼ Armeria juniperifolia 'Bevan's Variety'

I used this specimen to represent tufts of grass, though the plant bears white flowers in summer. The foliage curls attractively, echoing the roots of the crab apple tree. The rich green leaves contrast well with the variegated foliage of the thrift. There is one plant in this landscape.

▼ Moss

An attractive ground cover, moss is used to hide the planting medium. It also links the plantings of thrift, providing a pleasant, smooth, and natural finish that is perfectly in proportion to the scale of the landscape. See page 9 for suggestions on gathering and storing moss.

▼ Viola sylvestris

I find this dainty wood violet beautiful; in spring it has lovely, delicately scented purple flowers. I used two plants to extend the foreground beyond the limits of the container; the violets appear to fall over the rim. This texture and movement in the foreground adds a pleasing balance to the entire vista. Wood violet is an invasive plant that self-seeds readily; be sure to pinch off the flowers before they go to seed.

▼ Sedum hispanicum

To give a variety of color and texture I included three clumps of carpet-forming sedum with tiny gray succulent leaves and small starlike white flowers.

苹果

Ping Guo
PEACE

Jin Shi
METAL AND STONE

The dramatic Jin Shi landscape embraces the five essential elements in Eastern philosophy: water, metal, earth, fire, and wood. It is composed of a central white and silver rock flanked by metal beaches and surrounded by water. The rock, which appears to have been pushed up through the water by a volcanic eruption, stirs the inner self; at the same time, the water is calming. The metal reflects light and fire, and the waterfall cools the scenery. The entire picture is that of a dreamscape uniting the elements of the universe.

Eight false cypresses (*Chamaecyparis pisifera* 'Tsukumo') grow across the rock, and eight white horses, symbols of good luck and wisdom, are placed around it. In Far Eastern culture white has special significance: In Buddhism, white stands for loyalty and purity; in feng shui, the White Tiger that symbolizes the West is an animal of maturity and wisdom.

The fine trees with their rich, green foliage and red-brown trunks and branches rise from the earth and bring life to this silvery scene, which could be set in prehistoric times as much as the twenty-first century. To suggest a futuristic setting, I arranged it in a glass suiban, or water tray. I scattered glass chips in the suiban to add to the effect of the moving water, and used silver-coated pebbles to create beaches that appear to be made of metal.

setting up

Aluminum foil
A roll of ordinary kitchen foil is used in this project. Use it with the shiny side facing outward.

◀**Bonsai wire**
Copper-colored aluminum wire is available from bonsai suppliers. It is used for securing roots to the tray and for wiring branches.

▶**Mixing bowl**
A mixing bowl will be necessary for holding the ciment-fondu mixture.

Plastic sheeting
The sheeting is to protect your work surface and to wrap around the ciment-fondu rock. I split open trash-can liners and use those.

◀**Chinese watercolors**
I painted the rock with watercolors, which are surprisingly resistant to running when the landscape is watered. The colors fade in time, but meanwhile the rock takes on a patina of age.

▶**Chick grit**
Chick grit is a useful substitute for horticultural grit. It is finer and provides good drainage in a bonsai landscape.

Newspaper
Wrap the ciment-fondu rock in damp newspaper for 24 hours while it sets.

Large glass suiban
I used a rectangular suiban, or water tray, that measures approximately 18 by 12 inches (45 by 30cm).

▼**Paintbrush**
A brush that is about ½ to 1 inch (1 to 2.5cm) wide means the ciment fondu can be applied quickly and thickly. You also need a brush for applying the watercolors.

Constructing the landscape

The ciment-fondu rock in this futuristic landscape uses aluminum foil in its construction. It breaks through areas of the rock to give the appearance of lines of mineral ore. Wear a protective face mask when mixing and applying the ciment fondu.

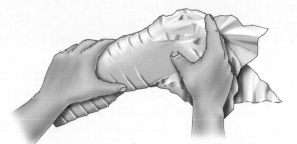

1 To make the rock, lay a sheet of aluminum foil, with the shiny side of the foil facing out, over a square of aluminum screening that is approximately 18 by 18 inches (45 by 45cm). Fold over the corners. Make 1-inch (2.5cm) pleats diagonally across the aluminum, then fan the pleats out in different places to mold the aluminum into the shape of the rock. (See pages 13–14.) The aluminum foil should be on the outside over the screening. Add texture to the rock face by sprinkling it with chick grit.

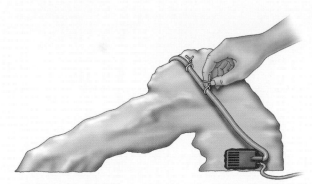

2 Position the plastic tubing for the water pump at the back of the rock and fasten the tubing to the rock with wire. Make sure the tube fits snugly to the pump adapter. Mix the ciment fondu in a bowl and then brush it over the entire piece of aluminum foil, leaving small areas of foil exposed. There should be silver lines and small irregular areas to simulate mineral ore in the rock. Cover the entire rock with damp newspaper or cloth and a plastic bag. Leave it to dry for 24 hours. When the rock has dried, if too much aluminum shows, cover some of it with plaster gauze. Again, allow the gauze to dry completely before proceeding.

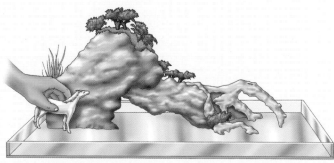

3 Paint parts of the rock green and add deep brownish-red tints to create shading. Allow the paint to dry. Position the rock in the suiban and use silicone glue to secure it in place, then glue the driftwood in position. Allow it to dry for 24 hours. After planting, the horses can be glued in place.

▼ Ciment fondu
Ciment fondu is available from building and masonry suppliers; it is also used for sculpting.

Plaster gauze
Available from art supply stores, this gauze, impregnated with plaster of paris, usually comes in 3-inch (7.5cm) wide strips.

Sphagnum moss
Chopped sphagnum moss is available from garden centers. It is a highly water-retentive planting medium.

▶ Water pump
Small water pumps are available at aquarium supply stores.

Akadama
Akadama is a general-purpose soil imported from Japan. It contains clay granules, which give it water-retentive properties.

◀ Silicone glue
This glue can be found at art and craft supply stores.

Sedge peat
This is an ideal planting medium for bonsai landscapes. When water is added to sedge peat, it becomes sticky and can be used to create planting pockets and bonsai pads (see page 14).

▶ Plastic tubing
This is connected to the water pump and threaded up through the rock so that the water flows over the rock.

▶ Aluminum screening
Pliable aluminum screening with pin-size holes is available in sheets from craft stores. You can apply ciment fondu directly to the screening.

Protective clothing
Wear gloves and a face mask when working with plaster and cement.

Bonsai soil mix
Available from specialty bonsai suppliers, this soil mix is one part loam, two parts spaghnum peat moss, and two parts granite grit.

Planting plan

Place all the plants toward the back of the landscape. Create planting pockets with sedge peat (see page 14) at the top of the rock and down the right-hand side. Place the two groups of false cypress with their bonsai pads into the planting pockets, then add akadama around the roots to allow air to circulate.

Cover the exposed areas of akadama with sedge peat wherever necessary to hold the planting together. Cover the soil with moss to prevent it from eroding when you water. Use sphagnum moss to create planting pockets on the left- and right-hand sides at the back of the landscape and fill the pockets with soil mix. Plant the two zebra rushes in the pockets.

Fit the pump into position, making sure it is not visible. Fill the suiban with rainwater. Use silver-coated pebbles to create metal beaches extending from both sides of the rock. Arrange the pebbles freely to add light and movement to the scene. Fill in the remaining area with glass chips to represent water.

Connect the water pump and adjust the settings so the water moves gently in the tray.

1. *Chamaecyparis pisifera* 'Tsukumo'
2. *Schoenoplectus lacustris* subsp. *tabernaemontani* 'Zebrinus'
3. Moss
4. White horses
5. Driftwood
6. Silver-coated pebbles
7. Glass chips

CARE

- **Positioning:** If the landscape will be kept indoors, it should be in an area that receives plenty of indirect sunlight but has no central heating. Outdoors, the leaves may scorch in hot sun, so it should be shielded. In cold climates, protect it from frost and harsh wind.
- **Watering:** Spray the landscape with water mornings and evenings.
- **Feeding:** Spray an organic liquid fertilizer as a foliar feed every 2 weeks from spring to fall. Follow the manufacturer's advice on dosage.
- **Pruning:** For the cypress, pinch back the growing shoots when the planting begins to look untidy. Remove the grass leaves of the zebra rushes as they die off.

the scenery

▲ **White horses**
Look for these graceful porcelain figurines at nurseries that specialize in bonsai plants. They are also available in terra-cotta clay that can be painted white. Select as many poses as possible to create a realistic effect.

▼ ***Schoenoplectus lacustris*** **subsp.** ***tabernaemontani*** **'Zebrinus'**
This miniature, reedlike grass is called zebra rush or club rush. It is widely available from garden centers and stores that carry aquarium plants. Its linear structure adds movement to the background and also provides perspective. You will need two plants for this landscape.

▲ **Glass chips**
I chose glass chips for this design because they provide an ideal base covering for any kind of container. Also, depending on the type of container you choose, glass chips provide texture and contrast. They are especially effective if you use a glass water tray.

▼ **Moss**
Introduce moss around the trees and zebra rush to cover any exposed soil or akadama. It adds an attractive finish to the planting. (See page 9 for suggestions on collecting moss.)

Group planting

Planting groups of trees so that they share one bonsai pad is an essential technique for bonsai landscapes. A group can consist of three to five trees, or you can attempt a forest group with a large number of trees planted together. Select species that have similar growing habits and foliage size.

1 ► I prepared my group plantings of false cypress with cuttings taken from one parent stock. Cuttings can be taken at any time during the growing season. The cuttings were grown for 1 year in a seed tray, then planted in a mixture of peat and sand in 3-inch (7.5cm) pots for another year.

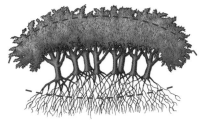

2 When the cuttings are approximately 2 years old, they can be removed from their pots. The roots are trimmed by one third and the branches are pruned back to 2 inches (5cm).

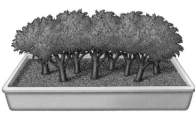

3 The plants can now be planted together in a seed tray to develop a unified bonsai pad. Spend some time placing the group, putting larger ones at the front and smaller ones at the back to create perspective.

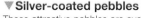

4 Let the trees grow for a year before removing them from the seed tray and root-pruning by one third again. At the same time, thin out the branches and cut away any that cross over each other. Keep the surface of the tray tilted if you intend the group to be placed on a slope.

5 The bonsai pad will take 3 to 4 years to form. Each year the roots and branches should be pruned by one third, until the pad is a solid, freestanding mass of roots.

► *Chamaecyparis pisifera* 'Tsukumo'

For this landscape, I used a Japanese dwarf variety of false cypress. *Chamaecyparis obtusa* 'Nana Gracilis' offers the same effect, even though it has slightly coarser foliage. I grew these eight young trees from cuttings. They provide the ideal proportion and perspective in the landscape. I often choose a plant for its color, as vibrant color brings life to a landscape. They are now around 3 years old. False cypress tolerates cool conditions by a well-lit window but should be shielded from full sun in summer, as the leaves will scorch.

▼ Silver-coated pebbles

These attractive pebbles are available in stores that carry aquarium supplies. In bonsai landscapes, algae tend to form on pebbles, but it's easy to clean these by removing them from the landscape and washing them in soapy water. Rinse them thoroughly. Silver is a neutral color that stabilizes the landscape design without detracting from the major aspects of the scene, and it also reflects light but recedes into the planting in shaded areas.

► Driftwood

You may be able to find a suitable piece of driftwood while at a beach. When you get home, wash the wood very thoroughly to leach out the salt; let it dry and bleach in the sun. You can also buy driftwood at garden centers and nurseries that specialize in bonsai plants. I chose a piece of pale wood with beautiful curves and gnarled, twisted projections, which I felt lent the perfect touch to this dreamscape.

金石

Jin Shi
METAL AND STONE

Lu Long
GREEN DRAGON

In this landscape, gnarled roots stretch over a cliff and out into the water, symbolizing the mighty green dragon Lu Long. The dragon is a symbol of male vigor and fertility—yang—and also traditionally signified the emperor, who is the son of heaven. Lu Long represents the East in feng shui and is also known as the blue-green dragon (Ging Long). He rises with the sun in the east, bringing fertility and spring rains to start the new growth of the season, as well as rain throughout the year. Here, he is symbolized by a Chinese elm *(Ulmus parvifolia)*, with its lush, green foliage (in Chinese philosophy, green represents growth).

In my landscape, the elm stands on the left. The design follows the tapering line of a naturally matured piece of wood, with the landscape planted in a half crescent. To create an illusion of depth, I paid careful attention to proportion while planting, setting miniature rhododendrons *(Rhododendron impeditum)*, moss, and grasses in the foreground and smaller plants on the mountaintop for a contrasting background.

A pot didn't seem right for this scene, so I used a piece of mature oak that looked as if it had been struck by lightning. I hollowed it out to become the container. It is a beautifully smooth piece with no blemishes. To give it the most stunning effect, I set it in a suiban, where the water reflects its full glory.

setting up

◀ Large rectangular suiban or water tray
Choose a suiban that is large enough to embrace most of the planting. The still water offers beautiful reflections of the tree above and also provides humidity for the plants.

▶ Akadama
Akadama is a general-purpose soil imported from Japan. It contains clay granules, which give it water-retentive properties. It can be sifted with sieves into coarse, medium, and fine grades.

◀ Leaf mold
Available from garden suppliers, leaf mold is made from leaves composted until they become a rich, crumbly humus, typical of forest floors.

◀ Chick grit
Chick grit is a useful substitute for horticultural grit. It is finer and provides good drainage in a bonsai landscape.

Plastic trash bag
The Chinese elm is a thirsty tree and the oak container is slightly porous, so I lined it with plastic to help it retain water.

Small wooden block (optional)
I used a small piece of wood to prop up the oak container in the suiban.

Constructing the landscape

This landscape is a simple, natural construction. Only one container was used—a piece of hollowed-out oak that offered numerous cavities for planting.

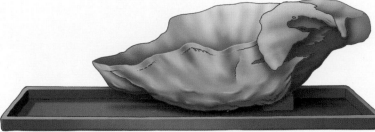

1 If you are lucky enough to have found a hollowed-out piece of wood suitable to be used as a container, clean off any debris from the outside of the wood and clean out the inside. If you buy a piece of wood from a bonsai supplier, it will have been cleaned already. Position the wood slightly off center in the suiban. If the wood is not freestanding, prop it up with a small block of wood. Fasten it in place with quick-drying cement, if necessary.

2 Line the oak container with a plastic bag (adjust the bag to the shape of the container so that it does not hang over the edge). The Chinese elm likes a lot of moisture and the liner helps prevent the container from drying out. The liner will be held in place by the weight of the sedge peat and the bonsai pad.

◀**Ericaceous soil mix**
This soil mix is essential for acid-loving plants, such as rhododendron.

◀**Sedge peat**
This is an ideal planting medium for bonsai landscapes. When water is added to sedge peat, it becomes sticky and can be used to create planting pockets and bonsai pads (see page 14).

▶**Sphagnum moss**
Chopped sphagnum moss is available from garden centers. It is a highly water-retentive planting medium.

▶**Quick-drying cement (optional)**
I used quick-drying cement to affix the oak container to the base of the suiban.

▲**Oak container**
You may be able to find an aged piece of oak from a fallen tree. This oak is a rich brown that contrasts well with the fresh green of the foliage. If you are unable to scavenge a piece of oak, you can buy a suitable piece from a bonsai supplier.

Planting plan

Prop up the oak container with a small block, and affix it to the suiban with cement. Fill the container's base with chopped sphagnum moss and chick grit, then put the Chinese elm in place. Add a moisture-retaining soil mix of two parts akadama, one part leaf mold, and one part chopped sphagnum moss around the roots. This elm is 25 years old and has been trained over time to have exposed roots. You can buy similar elms at bonsai suppliers, or you can train your own elm into an exposed-root style (see page 57).

Using an ericaceous soil mix suitable for rhododendrons, plant two of the rhododendrons in the foreground and one on the far right. Use sedge peat to form planting pockets (see page 14) to hold the rhododendrons in place, then put ericaceous soil mix around the roots.

Make planting pockets and plant the thyme raised behind the elm to look like a shrub on the mountaintop. For contrast, I planted azorella in the foreground. Thrift to the right of the elm echoes the curves of the knarled oak container. For all of these plantings, create sedge peat planting pockets (see page 14).

Add water to the suiban water tray to reflect the finished landscape and provide humidity for the planting. You can use tap water for this purpose.

1. *Ulmus parvifolia*
2. *Armeria maritima* 'Alba'
3. Oak container
4. *Thymus vulgaris*
5. *Rhododendron impeditum*
6. *Azorella trifurcata*

CARE

- **Positioning:** This landscape prefers to live outdoors, but would also do well in a sunny position in an unheated porch or vestibule.
- **Watering:** Chinese elms are water-loving trees, so do not allow them to dry out. Water once a day; during hot spells increase to twice a day. The other plants in the landscape should also be watered daily during the summer months. In winter, check the soil regularly and water before it dries out.
- **Feeding:** Apply pellets of organic bonsai fertilizer once a month.
- **Pruning:** Allow new growth on the elm to extend to four or five leaves, then prune to two sets of alternate leaves on the lateral shoots and one set of leaves at the top. Remove flowers from the rhododendrons as they fade, and remove new shoots after flowering. Trim and tidy the other plants, as needed.

the scenery

▲ *Thymus vulgaris*
Any species of thyme is suitable in this landscape. I used common thyme for its bushy form and dull, mid-green leaves. I positioned one plant on the right of the landscape to balance the scene.

▼ *Rhododendron impeditum*
The tiny mauve flowers and glossy green foliage of this dwarf rhododendron complement the dark oak container

beautifully. Because the plant has a tight rootball, I used it to help support the root system of the tree. After flowering, you should deadhead the spent flowers and trim off the last couple of leaves at the end of each branch. This reduces the size of the leaves and allows flower buds to form the following spring. The dwarf rhododendrons in the main photo are 2 to 3 years old. They require an acidic soil, so plant them in ericaceous soil mix. I used three plants in this landscape.

▲ *Armeria maritima* 'Alba'
White-flowered sea thrift looks very effective growing up the side of the oak container. It gives the appearance of long grasses growing on a mountainside. You will need one plant.

Foliage pads

The Chinese call foliage pads "steps to heaven," and this is exactly how they should appear. Visualize the branch as an outstretched hand, with the fingers of the hand supporting a cushion of foliage. This appearance is achieved by pruning using the following method.

1 ▶ Trees that are suitable for growing foliage pads can be trained to have closely spaced branches and compact foliage. Conifer, yew, rhododendron, pine, elm, and cotoneaster are all suitable. First thin out the branches, aiming for the traditional bonsai shape of an isosceles triangle, with longer branches at the base and the shortest at the apex.

2 If you wish, you can wire the main branch to increase its gnarled, aged appearance (see page 81).

3 As new growth appears, branches forming beneath and to the side of the main branch should be pruned away. Thin the upward-growing branches until you are left with a few strong shapes.

4 As the foliage thickens, keep pinching it back to 2 to 3 inches (5 to 7.5cm) above the main branch. Use the pads of your fingers rather than your fingernails, which can damage the foliage and cause browning on the pruned tips. Aim to prune into the shape shown above.

5 The foliage will slowly become a compact pad with the appearance of a much older tree. Continue to remove downward-hanging foliage as it grows, maintaining the ideal shape.

▶ *Ulmus parvifolia*

The fresh green foliage of Chinese elm attracts light and draws the eye. Its long, flexible roots and stout trunk lend it a natural, dragonlike form. The tree in the main photo is 25 years old. It has a beautiful tapering shape and no man-made scars. The tree is trained in the exposed-root style (see page 57).

▼ *Azorella trifurcata*

I used this as a ground cover in the foreground of the landscape. It is a compact, cushion-forming plant with tiny lobed leaves, ideal for a bonsai landscape. In summer it produces tiny yellow flowers. I used one plant in this landscape.

TIP

Azorella is excellent to use as an alternative to moss in the landscapes. Its lemony color among the plants creates an illusion of sunshine, while its raised surface provides interesting texture. Sprinkle chick grit around your azorella so that the stem of the plant is kept away from the damp ground.

Lu Long
GREEN DRAGON

綠
龍

梅花

Mei Hua
FLOWERING CHERRY

In late spring, the elegant flowering cherry bursts into a froth of pink flowers. Started from seed, the Japanese cherry (*Prunus serrulata* 'Kwanzan') in this landscape is about 14 years old. Its small leaves make a lovely frame for the exquisite blossoms. The red, weathered trunk has grown almost horizontally across the landscape, like a bridge linking two rocks. The strong lines of the trunk follow the contours of the rocks and valley until the tree thrusts forcefully upward, displaying its bouquet of blooms.

In China, Mei Hua, flowering cherry, is one of the three trees of winter; the other two are pine and bamboo. The cherry tree is hardy in winter and is one of the first trees to blossom in spring; the arrival of its blossoms heralds the warm weather to come. Blossom time in China and Japan is a much-loved season; it is hardly surprising that the petals of these beautiful flowers are also known as the "gods of good luck."

When creating this landscape, I made rocks out of ciment fondu to look like natural river rocks, evoking a far-off country vista. The simple lines of a shallow, unglazed container enhance the scene, which is reflected in the still water. The tray echoes the rich color of the cherry tree's bark.

setting up

◀Chick grit
Use this product as an alternative to horticultural grit.

▲Paintbrush
Ciment fondu can be applied with any brush. I find one that is about ½ to 1 inch (1 to 2.5cm) wide most suitable, as it means the mixture can be applied quickly and thickly.

Fiberglass cloth
Small sheets of fiberglass, readily available from craft stores, are layered onto the chicken-wire frame to create a nonporous base upon which the ciment fondu is applied.

◀Mixing bowl
A bowl is necessary for mixing the ciment fondu.

▶Sedge peat
This is an ideal planting medium for bonsai landscapes. When water is added to sedge peat, it becomes sticky and can be used to create planting pockets and bonsai pads (see page 14).

◀Wire cutters
You will need wire cutters to cut the chicken wire.

Newspaper
Wrap the ciment-fondu rock in damp newspaper and plastic until it has set.

Constructing the landscape

Spread a piece of plastic sheeting over the work surface. Wear protective gloves when working with the chicken wire and a face mask when mixing and applying the ciment fondu. In a bowl, mix up the ciment fondu according to the manufacturer's instructions.

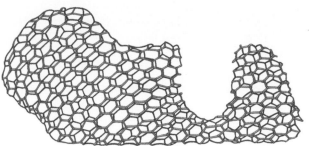

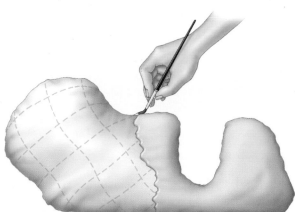

1 For this landscape, the goal is to create a steep, rocky mountain crag. Bend the chicken wire into your desired shape and mold it to include clusters of peaks and crevices with a valley in the middle. Make a deep crevice that is large enough to hold the rootball of the flowering cherry. Its cascade style means that it will have a fairly large rootball and will need a deep planting hole in order to stand upright.

2 Using a needle and thread, cover the chicken wire with the fiberglass cloth, then apply the ciment fondu with a paintbrush. (Follow the instructions on pages 13–14.) When the frame is covered with the ciment fondu, wrap it in damp newspaper, seal it with plastic, and leave it to set for 24 hours.

Place the ciment-fondu rock to the left of center in the suiban. This offset position provides a sense of height and perspective. Position the rock so that its most attractive face is visible from the front, and use quick-drying cement to affix it to the tray.

◀Chicken wire
Wire with a 1-inch (2.5cm) mesh is used to create the initial shape of the rocks.

Plastic sheeting
Use plastic sheeting to protect your work surface from the ciment fondu and to wrap round the ciment-fondu rock while it is setting.

▶Quick-drying cement
I use quick-drying cement to affix the rocks to the water tray.

Needle and thread
Use a strong sewing needle and thread for attaching fiberglass cloth to the chicken-wire framework of the rocks.

◀Rectangular suiban or water tray
I chose a handmade tray, which was a bright, terra-cotta color when new but has now dulled to a natural stone color.

▶Ciment fondu
Ciment fondu is used to create the solid bulk of the rock. It is strong and weather resistant yet much lighter than quick-drying cement.

◀Protective clothing
Wear gloves and a face mask when working with fiberglass cloth and cement.

Planting plan

The cherry tree is the most important plant in this landscape; think carefully about its position. You want to create a scene that evokes the moods of the changing seasons, so envision how you'll arrange the other plants around the cherry tree to create this effect.

The cascade-trained tree should have a raised rootball. Before planting it, remove some of the soil so the height of the rootball is lower than the height of the rock. Roll some balls of sedge peat to support the tree from underneath. Place the cherry tree on the tray with the sedge peat under it. Then position the lady's mantle against the tree's rootball. Use sedge peat to hold both plants firmly in place and to act as a container. Place two sorrel plants behind the cherry tree, and use sedge peat to fill in any gaps.

As you work toward the left part of the landscape, leave a gap where the valley will be. Make planting pockets with sedge peat, then plant two more sorrels—one in front of the tree and one behind it—and then plant the leptinella at the left front of the rock.

Plant the sedum along the edges of the rock on the left to soften the harsh lines, and add a clump of grass to the right of the landscape, if you wish. Arrange the moss to cover any exposed sedge peat and to add a smooth, verdant finish to areas where it seems appropriate. Dust any surface that is not covered with moss with chick grit.

1. *Prunus serrulata* 'Kwanzan'
2. *Oxalis vulcanicola* 'Sunset Velvet'
3. Grass
4. *Alchemilla ellenbeckii*
5. *Leptinella squalida*
6. *Sedum hispanicum*
7. Moss

CARE

- **Positioning:** The flowering cherry enjoys full sun. Protect it from frost in winter. When in flower, shield it from heavy rainfall.
- **Watering:** Water the landscape daily in summer. Avoid splashing the petals. In winter, water sparingly but do not let the soil dry out.
- **Feeding:** After flowering, feed with an organic bonsai fertilizer once a month until the beginning of fall.
- **Pruning:** After flowering, prune each stem of the cherry to an outward-facing bud. Flowers form on the previous year's wood.

the scenery

▼ *Sedum hispanicum*

The leaves of this sedum have a bluish tint and create a nice contrast against the hard edge of the rock. Use two plants.

▶ *Prunus serrulata* 'Kwanzan'

Although this cherry tree flowers for just a few weeks each year, its pink flowers create a spectacular display. I worked on the tree shown in the main photo for several years before planting it in the landscape. I grew it in a deep pot used for cascading bonsai (see page 111) to prevent the young tree from toppling over. Each year, I trimmed the cherry tree using the clip-and-grow method (see page 75); this allowed me to control the change of angle of the trunk. I started with a 6-year-old nursery tree and trained it using the clip-and-grow method for 8 years. Over time, this pruning method created a very gnarled tree. The tree is now 14 years old. Cherry trees benefit from an annual dressing of lime.

◀ *Alchemilla ellenbeckii*

I selected two clumps of miniature lady's mantle to refresh the landscape. The rich green leaves break up the pinks and oranges in the other planted areas. As well as providing lush ground cover, the plants help give perspective to the landscape. Lady's mantle thrives in moist, well-drained soil and does well in sun or partial shade. In summer, lime-green flowers appear, complementing the red trunk of the cherry tree.

Clip and grow

The flowering cherry in the Mei Hua landscape is pruned using the clip-and-grow method. This method entails cutting back branches and allowing new branches to form before cutting back again. An aged appearance is achieved quite quickly with this method, and the trunk tends to thicken nicely.

1 You can start this method when a tree is 2 years old, but I chose a 6-year-old tree that had a strong trunk. In the spring, I cut back the branches close to—but not right up to—the trunk. This is because the next year's growth will come from the pruned branches.

2 Allow the tree to grow without restriction for a year. This gives time for the trunk to thicken and take on character. After a year, cut back the new branches drastically and again allow the tree to grow for a year without pruning of any sort.

3 The following year, repeat the process, cutting off the previous season's growth. At this stage, unless you are also training the tree in cascade style, it should be root pruned and transferred to a seed tray so that it can begin to develop a bonsai pad.

4 Continue the yearly pruning in spring for 8 to 10 years. After that time, pruning can be reduced to once every other year. By this time, the tree will look much older than its true age and the trunk should be quite thick and gnarled.

▼ *Oxalis vulcanicola* 'Sunset Velvet'
Golden sorrel 'Sunset Velvet' is a newly available cultivar. It has the warm colors of sunset and is ideal for brightening niches among the rocks. I chose it to enhance the blush-pink blossoms of the cherry tree. This sorrel also sports tiny yellow flowers in summer. To grow well, it requires sandy, loamy soil. I used four plants in the landscape.

◀ *Leptinella squalida*
I used one of these delicate evergreen alpines from New Zealand; it resembles a miniature fern. In spring, tufts of new green growth break through the reddish-brown winter foliage, drawing the viewer's attention in close. The plant tolerates poor soil and prefers full sun. It has a creeping habit that makes it especially useful in a scene such as this one, where it provides an attractive alternative to moss for covering rocks.

▶ Grass
I added some lawn grass behind the lady's mantle as an afterthought. The grass provides an interesting contrast in leaf shapes that I think works very well.

◀ Moss
I collect moss from old brick walls and bridges, where it forms lovely flat tufts that look dry but turn a beautiful shade of green when soaked with water. You can also scrape moss off paving stones. Lay the moss on dry newspaper and cover it with more newspaper; you can store it this way until you need it for a landscape (see page 9).

Mei Hua
FLOWERING CHERRY

梅
花

Cai Shen
GOD OF RICHES

I named this landscape after Cai Shen, the Chinese deity associated with abundance, because of its lushness and the way the water and trees nourish each other. In the tradition of bonsai, the design contains elements that feng shui considers necessary to a home. A goldfish represents affluence, and there is a harmonious blend of mountains and water, yang and yin. Water flowing through a mountain creates positive energy, or *qi*. The trees are wired into "S" shapes to trap this energy. The invigorating rocks are situated in calming water, a fortunate juxtaposition and also horticulturally beneficial, as they conserve moisture essential for plants in a heated indoor environment. The inclusion of Chinese junipers (*Juniperus chinensis*) and artillery plants in the landscape is an excellent device for creating artificial perspective. The thick base of the juniper contrasts with the finely cut foliage of the artillery to give an impression of depth, as plantings that are further away appear to recede into the background.

setting up

◀ **Tray**
An ordinary terra-cotta tray is used, and it is painted gray to match the scenery. Make sure the tray is waterproof and deep enough so the pump can be submerged, and so fish can live in it.

Plastic sheeting
The sheeting is to protect your work surface and to wrap the ciment-fondu rock while it sets. I sometimes split open trash-can liners and use those.

▶ **River rock**
When choosing natural rocks look for ones whose character can be seen from every angle, and do not smother them with plants. In this scene, the main rock is made from ciment fondu, but the exposed rock on which the fisherman is sitting is real.

Fiberglass cloth
Fiberglass cloth covers the chicken wire before the ciment fondu is applied.

Terra-cotta paint
The tray is painted with gray terra-cotta paint.

Mixing bowl
You will need a mixing bowl for making up the ciment fondu.

▼ **Paintbrush**
One paintbrush is needed to paint the terra-cotta tray and another to apply the mixed ciment fondu to the fiberglass cloth.

▶ **Ciment fondu**
Ciment fondu provides the solid bulk of the waterfall. It is a useful medium favored by sculptors for outdoor statues because it is strong and weather resistant.

▶ **Quick-drying cement**
I use quick-drying cement to affix the ciment-fondu rock to the water tray.

Needle and thread
Use a strong needle and thread to attach the fiberglass cloth to the chicken-wire framework.

Constructing the landscape

Start by making a sketch of your landscape. Spread a piece of plastic sheeting on your work surface. Wear protective gloves when working with the chicken wire and a face mask when mixing and applying the ciment fondu. As you create your rock shape with the chicken wire, remember to provide a cavity where you can hide the water pump.

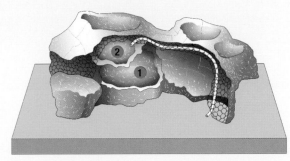

1 Mold chicken wire into a half-crescent shape. Make two shell-shaped pieces of chicken wire, one smaller than the other, and attach them to the chicken-wire frame with wire (see 1 and 2 in the diagram above). Thread the tubing that will run from the pump through the chicken wire to emerge at the waterfall outflow at the top left-hand corner. Make a crevice so that the pump can be hidden; press in areas of the wire to create planting pockets. With a needle and thread, sew the fiberglass cloth all over the chicken wire.

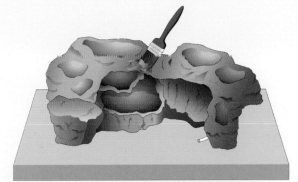

2 In a mixing bowl, mix the ciment fondu according to the package directions, then apply it to the fiberglass cloth with a paintbrush. Make sure that the end of the tubing at the waterfall outflow is covered and disguised by the ciment-fondu rock.

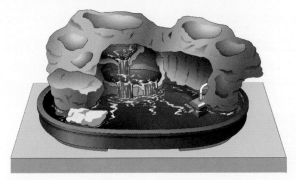

3 When the rock formation is complete, cover it with damp newspaper, wrap it in a damp cloth, and leave it to dry for 24 hours. While the ciment fondu is setting, paint the tray. When it is dry and the rock has set, attach the entire frame to the tray with quick-drying cement. Connect the water pump to the tubing, and run the electric wire around the back of the landscape. Test the water pump and then tuck it out of sight. Position the river rock.

Sedge peat
When planting trees clasped to rocks, sedge peat is an ideal medium. Alternatively, use a sticky mixture of half peat and half clay blended with water. The mixture will help the roots stick to the rock and will harden after 12 hours or so.

▶Protective clothing
Wear gloves and a face mask when working with wire, fiberglass cloth, and cement.

▶Chicken wire
This forms the structural base of the design. A more open gauge will add character to your landscape, a finer gauge is easier to control.

Bonsai wire
This can be used to link chicken wire pieces.

Wire cutters
Wire cutters are needed to cut the bonsai wire and chicken wire.

Newspaper
Wrap the ciment-fondu rock in damp newspaper and seal it with plastic while it sets.

▶Water pump
You need an electric water pump with an adjustable flow of water. Because the pump must be completely covered, its size will define the depth of the tray—with smaller, modern pumps you can use shallower trays, which are more aesthetically pleasing.

Akadama
Akadama is a general-purpose soil imported from Japan. It contains clay granules, which give it water-retentive properties.

◀Plastic tubing
The tubing will carry the water from the water pump to the waterfall outflow.

Planting plan

In the indents made for the plants, make planting pockets with sedge peat (see page 12). Sprinkle akadama in the base of each pocket, then plant the cuttings of 'Nana' along the top of the crescent, to the left, right, and center. Plant two Chinese junipers on the left, toward the front of the landscape, and three on the right. Dot the artillery plants around areas of open rock at the top of the landscape to soften the outline of the rock. Place the sweet flag at the edge of the rock, where its long leaves will be reflected in the water, and plant the liverwort nearby. The moss will grow on any exposed rock.

When you are happy with the planting, fill the tray with rainwater or bottled water and turn on the pump. When the water is running gently, place the goldfish in the water.

CARE

- **Positioning:** This landscape thrives in a cool northeast-facing environment, where it receives sun only in the early morning. Because of the goldfish, the landscape should be kept indoors in an unheated room.
- **Watering:** Mornings and evenings, spray thoroughly with a plant sprayer until the landscape is completely saturated.
- **Feeding:** Do not feed this landscape, as it will harm the fish. Once every two months, empty half the water into a bowl and then feed that to the plants—the sediment acts as a fertilizer. Top off the bowl with rainwater or bottled water.
- **Pruning:** The junipers and artillery plants should all be plucked with the fingers to maintain a tight triangular shape. The sweet flag will grow too long in time and should be removed and replaced.

1. *Juniperus chinensis*
2. *Juniperus procumbens* 'Nana'
3. *Pilea microphylla*
4. *Acorus gramineus*
5. *Lunularia cruciata*
6. Moss
7. River rock
8. Fisherman

the scenery

▼ Moss
Any kind of moss will do here, but look for moss growing on a good soil base. Moss is usually purchased in ¼-in (6mm) pieces, but it can also be gathered. The best time to harvest moss is in the spring; store it in a cool place between layers of newspaper, then revive it when you are ready to plant by spraying it with rainwater (see page 9).

▲ Goldfish
Goldfish thrive in shallow water and add a new dimension to any landscape. Use only rainwater, never tap water. It is better not to feed them with normal aquarium flakes, as they can foul the water; floating pellets are a good alternative.

▼ *Lunularia cruciata*
Liverwort is commonly found in poorly drained flowerpots, where it can prevent rain from penetrating to plants' roots. Here, though, the ten clumps help hold the planting medium in place.

▶ *Acorus gramineus*
Sweet flag is a cultivated bog grass, easily obtained from most aquarium stores. It prefers cool, damp conditions and partial shade. Its fan-shaped tufts echo the shape of the water flowing over the rock. The normal length of the blades is reduced by one third because of the shallow depth of the soil.

Wiring trees

Trees can be made into almost any shape with the aid of wiring. You can use either copper or aluminum. Aluminum sets the branches better and is less harmful to bonsai soil. Early spring is the best time for deciduous trees. Evergreens can be wired any time, but only wire conifers in winter, when they are dormant.

1 ▶ For maximum branch flexibility, don't water your tree for 24 hours before wiring. Choose a wire gauge one third the diameter of the branch or trunk to be wired. Before cutting a length, measure your wire against the branch or trunk to be wired, then add one third again. Begin with the trunk, anchoring the wire securely at the base.

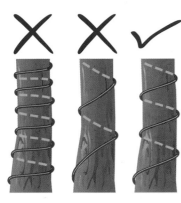

2 Wind the wire once horizontally around the base of the trunk before winding it neatly up the trunk at a 45-degree angle. Wire toward the front, not too tight and not too loose, just so it is touching the bark's surface. Never cross the wire and always wire in the same direction.

3 Wire the primary branches, starting with the lowest. Work in pairs, anchoring the wire on the trunk. To prevent the branch from snapping, ensure the wire's first turn is over the branch. Don't wire over foliage or small branches. For drastic bends on big branches, first protect them with raffia, or a foam pad.

4 Adjust the branch positions. If any wiring is too loose the branch may break when bending. If a branch doesn't break off completely, you can stick it back on with garden tape.

5 Leave the tree for 6 to 12 months, checking regularly that the wire is not cutting into the bark. Autumn is the best time to remove the wire, especially for pines. Starting with the tips of the branches, remove the wire very carefully, by cutting rather than uncoiling it. Paint any wounds with sealant.

▼ *Juniperus chinensis*
Both the Chinese and the Japanese have used this variety of conifer in their displays for centuries. The trunks and branches can be wired into wonderful shapes. To groom this juniper, you should pluck the foliage rather than pinch out the needles. Only prune the second year's woody growth. You will need five plants here.

▶ *Juniperus procumbens* 'Nana'
Plant several cuttings of Japanese mound juniper in seed trays in early summer and pot them up the following spring. To prepare for rock planting, group them together on small pieces of slate so they develop a bonsai pad.

◀ *Pilea microphylla*
Artillery plant originated in Central America and thrives in moist conditions. It must be protected from frost. Propagate from ½-inch (12mm) cuttings inserted in horticultural sand. When root growth starts, trim or pluck to the desired shape, then plant in your bonsai garden.

▼ Yu Fu—Fisherman with Fish
Shiwan figures from China are handcrafted from a lump of clay. They add color to the landscape and tame the wilderness. The fisherman, with his rod and line, also suggests to the viewer the presence of the fish under the rocks. In fact, as soon as the pump is turned on, the goldfish appear and the whole scene bursts into action.

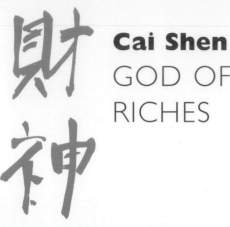

Cai Shen
GOD OF RICHES

MOSS
AT A GLANCE

✤ As well as looking good, moss helps the soil retain water and keeps it compact in its container. Use it sparingly, and always keep it away from the edge of the pot, or it can stop water from getting to the soil.

✤ Many mosses are suitable to use in bonsai. They are particularly popular in group plantings, where different textures can give subtle impressions of depth.

✤ You can buy tubs of Japanese mountainside moss spores, or grow your own. After gathering wild moss, preferably in the autumn when natural growing conditions are ideal, leave it to dry out over several days. Then crumble it through a sieve and mix with a little soil before sprinkling a handful to cover the exposed areas of a landscape. Keep moist and shaded, and after a season the moss will have grown again.

Yin Meng Yang
YIN DREAMS OF YANG

This restful landscape depicts a Japanese lady with an umbrella sheltering from the passing rain beneath a Sawara cypress (*Chamaecyparis pisifera* 'Boulevard') twin-trunk tree. While she waits, she dreams of her future. This is depicted by the ornate pagoda on the right side of the landscape. Behind the Japanese lady, her past is connected to the future by a stone bridge. Over the bridge, memories of her childhood home— full of bright sunshine—are depicted by the lemon-yellow cypress trees (*Cupressus macrocarpa* 'Goldcrest').

In Chinese philosophy, yin—the feminine—is represented by shade, rain, cold, and shelter. In contrast, yang—the masculine—is represented by happiness, warmth, energy, and the gods. I have suggested all these elements in my scene: the yin of the Japanese lady who dreams of the yang of the sunlit trees of her childhood home and the security of her future.

My two groups of cypress trees provide shade and shelter. The pagoda represents a future home filled with happiness. As she leaves behind childhood and youthful energy, our Japanese lady goes in search of an understanding of yin and yang. She stands beside a stream, represented by fine sharp sand, which draws the viewer's eye into the undulating curves of the planting.

setting up

▶ Paints
You may need gray metal primer (available from car accessory stores) and watercolor paints in neutral gray and alizarin crimson to tone down and age the finish on your figurines and ornaments. To add details to the Japanese lady, you will need model paints, such as Humbrol Super Enamel color 148 for a skin tone, and a creamy-yellow gloss paint, such as color 200.

Turpentine
Use turpentine to clean your paintbrushes after they have been used for model paints.

▲ Artists' paintbrushes
Use medium paintbrushes to tone down and age your ornaments, and a size no. 1 or no. 2 fine paintbrush for the details on the Japanese lady.

▼ Sedge peat
Use this to create planting pockets in the landscape (see page 14).

Glass tray
You will need a large, shallow glass tray, approximately 12 by 24 inches (30 by 60cm) and 1¾ inches (4.5cm) deep. You may be able to custom order one from an aquarium store. If you do, make sure the joins are as clean as possible.

Styrofoam
Support your glass tray on Styrofoam while you work on it, as it will crack if it is on an uneven surface or if there are traces of grit beneath it.

Constructing the landscape

It is worth taking the time to search for interesting, unusual ornaments; I found my Japanese hut and Japanese lady in an antiques market. Selecting and positioning your trees and ornaments thoughtfully is the first step to creating a successful design.

① While you work, leave the glass tray supported on Styrofoam to prevent cracking. Use paints and an artist's paintbrush to tone down the brightness of the ornaments and add a patina of age.

② Decide where your trees and ornaments should be positioned. Mark the positions of the root pads and the bases of the ornaments using sharp sand. When you are happy with the position of the ornaments, squeeze a drop of silicone glue onto each position in the tray and a drop onto each ornament. Use a piece of slate chip to raise the height of the Japanese lady, the hut, and the pagoda. Next, glue the ornaments to the slate, then glue the slate pieces to the glass. Allow to set. This will probably take 1 hour.

▶ Horticultural sharp sand

This sand is used by Japanese women to make dry landscape designs, and the results are breathtakingly beautiful. It is a very fine sand, which I find represents water convincingly in a landscape. Here I have used it to depict the stream. The sand at the front shows through the glass tray, suggesting depth to the water, and it also appears to flow toward the viewer. Sharp sand is also used to mark the positions of the trees and ornaments in the landscape.

◀ Florist's wire

Green florist's wire is used to join the group of cypresses.

◀ Silicone glue

Use the same type of silicone glue that was used to construct the glass tray to adhere the ornaments to the tray. Do not use superglue, as it cannot be removed if you make a mistake.

▲ Akadama

Use coarse akadama as drainage material at the base of the planting pockets.

▲ Slate chip

You can use any kind of stone chips to create stepping-stones in the landscape, but slate chips have a perfect color that blends in with the plants and ornaments. If you use chips of another color, make sure they are as natural as possible and try to tone your ornaments to match.

Planting plan

In this landscape, the two twin-trunk style (see page 87) Sawara cypresses give height and balance to the scene. The trees I used have firm, thick root formations that have been built up to this height over 6 years. I placed a layer of akadama on the base of the tray and placed the freestanding trees on top. If your trees have shallow bonsai pads or are unsteady, secure them with sedge peat planting pockets (see page 14). Fill the areas between the bonsai pads with more sedge peat so that you can plant the other plants. Plant the two 'Goldcrest' cypresses on the left of the scene, behind one of the twin-trunk trees, and plant the small group of 'Goldcrest' cypresses to the right of the landscape.

Plant moss and the 'Tsukumo' cypress beside the pagoda. I used grassy-leaved sweet flag below the Japanese lady to enhance the groundwork and added pilea to the front of the scene on the right-hand side. Cover exposed areas of the banks with moss. Finally, pour sand beneath the bridge and toward the front of the landscape so that it creates a pool close to the edge of the tray, giving the effect of flowing water.

CARE

- **Positioning:** The landscape can be placed indoors in a cool place with plenty of light and air movement. A kitchen window would be ideal.
- **Watering:** The soil mix must be kept moist. You can check the water level through the sides of the glass tray. Indoor cultivation needs extra care, so make sure you mist the landscape overhead every morning and evening, using rainwater at room temperature.
- **Feeding:** Apply pellets of organic bonsai fertilizer from May to October.
- **Pruning:** Use the plucking method—remove half the growing tips of new foliage with your fingers.

1. *Chamaecyparis pisifera* 'Boulevard'
2. *Cuppressus macrocarpa* 'Goldcrest'
3. *Chamaecyparis pisifera* 'Tsukumo'
4. *Pilea microphylla*
5. Moss
6. *Acorus gramineus*
7. Ornaments

the scenery

▶ *Cuppressus macrocarpa* **'Goldcrest'**

This conifer is available in most garden centers. For the two individual plantings, I used trees from 3-year-old stock that I had previously root pruned. I reduced the height of the trees and gently wired the branches outward, trimming them into a triangular pattern. For the group I used six 3-year-old cuttings that were still in little pots. I removed the trees and linked them together with wire to make them more managable.

▶ *Chamaecyparis pisifera* **'Boulevard'**

I chose this Sawara cypress for its lovely bluish tinge. I have root pruned and trimmed these two groups of trees over 8 years to create the illusion of old trees that have stood on that piece of ground for a long time. You can start a landscape with trees that are 3 years old. You will need two trees in the twin-trunk style for this landscape.

▶ *Pilea microphylla*

I used artillery plant in this scene because the plant clips well and looks like the clipped azaleas you see in Japanese gardens. Don't throw the clippings away, as they will root readily in a water tray, ensuring you have a ready supply for making other landscapes. If you have difficulty locating *P. microphylla*, *Selaginella kraussiana* also works well. You will need two plants in this landscape.

▶ *Chamaecyparis pisifera* **'Tsukumo'**

This tree has very fine foliage and can be used in a landscape from a young age. At 2 years old, it can be used to represent distant mountain "pines." Use one tree here.

Twin-trunk style

Single trees can be married together to produce a twin-trunk style. Work on the trees individually by root and branch pruning until they both have close internodes throughout. The internode is the length of stem between two leaf joints. To plan the branch placement, follow the method for informal upright style (see page 21).

1 ▶ When you have prepared the two trees, place the tree roots together, making sure they look as if they have always grown this way. Plant them in a small pot so that their root systems will become entwined. They will then share one bonsai pad, which is essential for this landscape. You may need to bind them in the pot with raffia to secure them in position while you wire them.

2 Remove branches that are crossing each other. You need just six or seven branches to form an attractive tree. The trees are now ready to be wired into shape.

3 Arrange the branches in a triangular pattern. The lower branches should always appear longer and heavier, with the upper branches lighter and "bouncing" upward. To create this effect, pull less of the wired branches downward as you move up the tree.

4 In nature, the apex, or crown, of the tree strives to tower over other trees to get maximum exposure to light, and it is normally flat with a spray of smaller branches. For this bonsai tree to remain healthy, you will need to restrict the apex, otherwise the lower branches will die.

5 The combined bonsai pad will have formed after approximately 2 years. Once a year, take the trees out of the pot, prune the roots by one third, then dip them into a wet mixture of sedge peat before returning them to the pot. This tends to concentrate the root hairs and produce a smaller pad.

▶ Metallic Japanese lady

When you buy ornamental figures they are often painted in subdued colors. However, I prefer an old-fashioned look, and this can be achieved by painting details on the figure. Using model paint in a skin tone, paint the flesh areas of the figurine. Paint the collar and sash with the creamy yellow gloss paint. Make sure you clean your brushes in turpentine after use.

Ornaments

I found my delightful Japanese hut and the Japanese lady with the umbrella in an antique market. They are typical of most Japanese ornaments and are made of metal. The large pagoda is made of brass, which needed to be toned down by spraying it with gray metal primer. Then, I painted it with a muddy mixture of soil and water. I bought the molded cement bridge from an aquarium store. I painted it with watercolor paints in neutral gray and alizarin crimson to give it a lovely slate-gray color.

▼ *Acorus gramineus*

I used two clumps of grassy-leaved sweet flag, a grasslike perennial that brings movement to the scene and softens the ground in front of the Japanese lady.

▲ Moss

Use any type of moss you can find in the garden or growing in parks or the countryside. A variety of types will add interest to the scene.

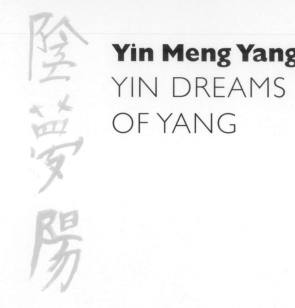

Yin Meng Yang
YIN DREAMS OF YANG

FALSE CYPRESS
AT A GLANCE

🌿 False cypress *(Chamaecyparis pisifera)* are native to Japan and North America, and two species in particular lend themselves to bonsai. Hinoki cypress *(C. obtusa)* and Sawara cypress *(C. pisifera)* both have attractive foliage and interesting bark.

🌿 These evergreens have fan-shaped branches bearing scalelike foliage that ranges in color from deep green to blue-gray depending on the species. They are hardy and long-lived, tolerate pruning, and are easily grown from cuttings.

🌿 Provide good light but do not leave them in full sun in the height of summer, when the leaves will scorch. Water daily to ensure the soil does not dry out, but do not saturate, as they do not like too much water.

観立目

Quan Yin
BAMBOO RETREAT

A bamboo stem is one of the emblems of the Chinese god Quan Yin. It symbolizes wisdom and old age, and when the wind blows, it bends in laughter. There is a legend that Quan Yin transformed himself into a goddess to help a woman in childbirth. Since that time, Quan Yin has been known as the Goddess of Mercy.

This peaceful bamboo landscape is a retreat for quiet contemplation. I have made boulders to surround the plantings and added to the tranquil vista by using sand to represent water flowing around the rocky island. A boulder bridge connects the two sides of the landscape, and water flowing beneath it beckons the viewer into the depths of the grove.

Three groves of bamboo complete the scene. The tallest bamboo, *Phyllostachys aureosulcata* 'Spectabilis,' waves gracefully on the right. A group of medium-sized bamboo, *Pleioblastus gramineus*, sets off an ancient Chinese lantern, its roof clothed in the artillery plant *Pilea microphylla*. The smallest groups of bamboo are the more common *Bambusa multiplex*. Some of their stems spiral up to the sky. The slate used for the base gives the illusion of flat, open ground and makes the handmade rocks appear larger than they are. This landscape can be kept indoors as long as it has cool, moist conditions.

setting up

Plastic sheet
Cut a rectangle of plastic sheet the same size as the wooden shelf.

◀Scissors
You will need regular scissors to cut the aluminum and plaster gauze into squares, as well as small, sharp bonsai scissors.

Pencil
The wired bamboo is wound around a pencil to train it into a spiral.

▼Plaster gauze
This is a useful material for making rock formations that will be kept indoors, as it is not frost-proof. Cut eight 2-inch (5cm) squares of plaster gauze, then cut each piece diagonally. The completed boulder is a good representation of sandstone and is very porous. Because the landscape will receive regular misting, moss will easily form on the wet surface of the boulders.

▼Paintbrush
A medium-sized artist's paintbrush is ideal for applying watercolors to the lantern.

▶Watercolor paints
You will need sap green and alizarin crimson watercolor paints to tone down the hue on a new Chinese lantern.

▶Bonsai wire
Use this to wire the extended growth of the bamboo to form a spiral shape and to support the bamboo during pruning.

Aluminum gauze
You will need aluminum gauze to form the boulders.

Mixing bowl
You will need a bowl to mix the quick-drying cement and sharp sand.

Constructing the landscape

Handmade "sandstone" boulders are easy to make and light in weight. Moss will soon grow on their moist, porous surfaces, making them appear realistic. Wear protective gloves and a face mask when working with concrete.

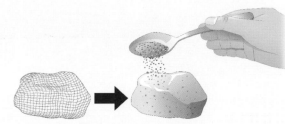

1 To make the boulders (see pages 12–13), cut the aluminum gauze with scissors into three squares in the following sizes: 4 inches (10cm), 3 inches (7.5cm) and 2 inches (5cm). Then pleat the squares slightly. Form the pleated aluminum gauze into boulder shapes by fanning out some areas and pressing into the center of others. Cover the boulders with the pieces of wet plaster gauze. While the gauze is wet, use a spoon to sprinkle some quick-drying cement and sand mixture onto it. Repeat the process for the other rocks. Leave them for a day to set.

2 Lay the plastic sheet on the wooden shelf. Place the two roof slates on the plastic sheet. Run a line of silicone glue along the center join of the two slates and press the edges together. The glue will take about 2 hours to set. Place your three groups of bamboo plantings on the slates and mark around them with the horticultural sharp sand. Remove the bamboo plantings.

3 When the rocks are dry, arrange them on the slate base around the areas you have marked for the bamboo so that they make a natural landscape. Create a slightly off-center boulder bridge spanning two boulders. Glue the rocks in place with silicone glue when you are happy with the arrangement. Allow 2 hours for the glue to set.

Lantern platform
The lantern needs to be raised above the boulders. You can use anything that is approximately 2 inches (5cm) high, such as a bowl.

◀ **Roof slates**
Two roof slates make the perfect base for this landscape. They will be joined with silicone glue and supported on a slatted wooden shelf.

◀ **Horticultural sharp sand**
I used white sharp sand to give an illusion of flowing water. It is also used for marking the position of the plantings.

▶ **Quick-drying cement**
Cement is mixed 50:50 with horticultural sharp sand and sprinkled over the plaster-gauze boulders.

▶ **Silicone glue**
Use silicone glue to join the slates and to attach the boulders and lantern to the slate base.

Slatted wooden shelf
You will need a shelf to support the roof slates. It needs to be just slightly smaller than the joined tiles so that it is not easily visible.

Spoon
You will need this for applying quick-drying cement.

▶ **Protective clothing**
Always wear protective gloves and a dust mask when working with concrete.

Sedge peat
This soil is ideal for bamboo, which needs moist conditions.

Planting plan

Begin with the small bamboo *(Bambusa multiplex)*. When you remove it from the pot, you will find a mass of new growth, which is a beige color. Wire this growth with bonsai wire, then wind the wired bamboo around a pencil so that it spirals upward. When you release the wire, the stem of bamboo will have formed a corkscrew. Do this for all the extended growth and leave it wired for one growing season—approximately 6 months.

Using bonsai scissors, trim the root hairs spiraling along the internodes of the bamboo from the pale underground bamboo growth. Remove excess soil mix from the bonsai pads, let dry, then soak the roots with wet sedge peat before fitting the pads into the boulders glued on the left side of the slate. Fill any gaps with more sedge peat. Paint the lantern with watercolors, then raise it on a platform between the two plantings of bamboo. Use silicone glue to secure the lantern and platform to the slate. Position the medium-sized bamboo *(Pleiobastus gramineus)* at the back, to the right of the Chinese lantern. Remove the two groups of the large bamboo *(Phyllostachys aureosulcata)* from their pots and carefully tidy the bonsai pads. Place them in two groups on the roof slate at the right of the landscape.

Position the sedum, mint, and fuchsia around the landscape, and plant the pilea on the roof of the lantern. Add sand around the perimeter of the rocks to give the appearance of water flowing around an island. Pour sand under the boulder bridge so it appears that water is flowing into the landscape and beyond.

1. *Phyllostachys aureosulcata* 'Spectabilis'
2. *Fuchsia microphylla*
3. *Mentha requienii*
4. *Sedum hispanicum*
5. *Pleioblastus gramineus*
6. *Pilea microphylla*
7. *Bambusa multiplex*
8. Chinese lantern

CARE

- **Positioning:** This landscape can be placed indoors or out. If situated indoors, select a cool well-lit place, such as a northwest-facing windowsill. It will tolerate a couple of hours of direct sun each day. If situated outdoors, choose a position in dappled shade. If the landscape receives 2 hours of direct sun each day, make sure it is well watered.
- **Watering:** Keep moist at all times. Curled leaves are an indication of drought. Spray overhead with rainwater morning and evening, and do not allow the soil mix to dry out.
- **Feeding:** This is a hungry landscape planting. Organic bonsai fertilizer is simple to use, because you imbed the granules in the soil mix and the food is slowly released for the plants to use.
- **Pruning:** To reduce the height of the stems, carefully half-peel the sheaths that cover them (see instructions on page 93).

the scenery

▼ Sedum hispanicum
In spring, *S. hispanicum* displays a lovely network of delicate branches that give a sense of age to the landscape. I used ten clumps here.

▼ Phyllostachys aureosulcata 'Spectabilis'
This attractive bamboo is not too large to be tamed. The internodes are marked at alternate intervals. The stems are a lovely orange-yellow color. You will need two clumps with several stems for the landscape. This bamboo needs overhead spraying in the spring and summer months to flourish. Spray mornings and evenings.

▼ Mentha requienii
A tiny purple-flowered mint, this plant creeps along the ground and gives a soft texture to the landscape. The plant flowers toward the end of spring and into early summer. Here, I used four plants.

▶ Pleioblastus gramineus
This species of bamboo is native to Japan, and its elegant growth habit makes it a favorite for bonsai landscapes. I find it likes a fair amount of water, so I tend to grow it in bog conditions. This plant was taken from the parent plant in my garden and has been growing in a porcelain bowl for 2 years. You will need one clump for this landscape, with around nine stems.

Peeling bamboo culms

A bamboo cane is known as a culm. The sheaths are the outer layers of growth on the bamboo culm. When they are peeled you will see water escape. This is from the supply that encourages upward growth. By releasing the water, you deplete the supply to the plant, and this will slow down the growth.

1 ▶ Before you begin, be aware that this is a difficult, delicate process. The culm is extremely soft and tender and is easily damaged. It is also easy to snap the new growth. Beginning at the base of the culm, make a small incision in the sheath.

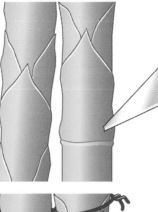

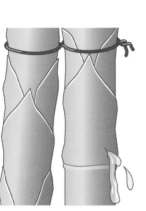

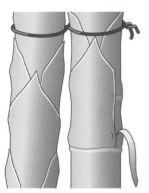

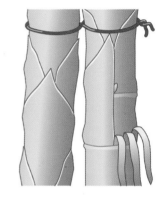

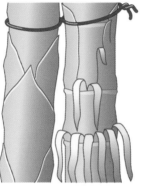

2 Water will gush out, making the top heavier than the bottom. You are left with limp bamboo. Be careful it doesn't flop over. Prop it up by tying it to the next cane with some very fine wire.

3 Gently slice a strip up the culm with your fingernail. Remove the strip very, very slowly over the course of a day. Keep returning and pull back the tiniest bit more. If you have the patience, doing this over the course of 2 days is even better.

4 Peel away the sheath, strip by strip, very slowly over a period of days. Continue until the whole of the sheath is hanging loose. Do not tear off the strips since it is very easy to cause damage to the fragile culm.

5 You will need to monitor growth daily and repeat the peeling process until the stem has reached the height you require. You may need to prop up the growth with a fine piece of bonsai wire when you reach the top, as it will not have support from the sheaths and may start to bend.

▼ Chinese lantern
You can buy a terra-cotta lantern from a Chinese gift store. Try to obtain one that is about 3 inches (7.5cm) high to add to the planting of *Bambusa multiplex*. The lantern I used in this project was white, so I used watercolor paints to age it.

▼ *Pilea microphylla*
I used an artillery plant in this scene to cover the roof of the Chinese lantern. If you have difficulty locating it, *Selaginella kraussiana* also work well.

▼ *Bambusa multiplex*
This is a fairly invasive plant when grown in the garden, so it is best to grow it in a container. The plants shown here were taken from the parent plant in my garden and have been in a container for two years. A glass dish is useful for housing cuttings, as you can monitor the water level simply by looking through the glass. You will need three clumps for the landscape.

▼ *Fuchsia microphylla*
This fuchsia has very small pink flowers, which are borne on the tips of the foliage pad in summer. I used it to add color and summer interest to the landscape. It likes plenty of light. Protect it from frost.

Quan Yin
BAMBOO
RETREAT

BAMBOO
AT A GLANCE

❧ A member of the grass family, bamboo grows wild in Asia, predominantly in China and Japan. For bonsai, bamboo is usually planted in groups. The best genera for this are *Arundinaria*, *Sasa,* and *Phyllostachys.*

❧ Bamboo is a fast-growing plant, so growth control is very important. You do this by removing culms, root pruning, cutting above a node, or cutting at soil level.

❧ Bamboo likes partial shade and a well-drained mix of soil. Water daily and feed with a high-nitrogen fertilizer every 2 weeks in spring and summer.

龍樹龜水

Long Shu Gui Shui
DRAGON TREE, TORTOISE POND

The dramatic Long Shu Gui Shui landscape depicts the Chinese symbol of male vigor and fertility—yang—in the form of a dragon. Spring rain wakes the sleeping dragon and it soars into the air, spreading its wings. A tortoise watches nearby and is so delighted by the spectacle that it turns over onto its back, creating a pool beneath the dragon's outspread wings. All the plants in the scene join in the spring celebration.

    The dragon and tortoise are both celestial animals. The dragon represents fertility and is a positive force in feng shui. He is depicted here in the form of a twisted 50-year-old pomegranate *(Punica granatum).* In Chinese philosophy, the tortoise holds the secret of heaven and Earth and is represented here in the form of a pond created from a naturally scooped piece of Canadian lace rock. Two other pieces of lace rock complete the scene of an eroded cliff face, with a lush planting over a gentle slope. A fig tree *(Ficus nerifolia)* leans over the pond, as if gazing at its reflection in the water. Miniature rhododendrons *(Rhododendron impeditum)* and grasses grow around the pond. A large rectangular handmade ceramic water tray holds the landscape. Its straight lines contrast with the twisting, irregular shapes of the pomegranate and fig trees and the blue-gray rocks.

setting up

▼Tray
I commissioned a potter to make me a handmade tray. It measures approximately 12 by 36 inches (30 by 90cm) by 1 inch (2.5cm) deep and is unglazed.

▶Canadian lace rocks
You will need three rocks. I was able to purchase perfectly shaped rocks for this landscape from a specialty marine aquarium store. One of the rocks also has a natural reservoir to contain the pond. Lace rock has many cracks and crevices and some patches of natural yellow lichen growing on it. Its gray color has a green tint when wet.

◀Coarse grit
Use this grit in the bottom of the tray for drainage. Different grades of grit are available from most garden centers. Always rinse it before using.

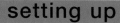

▼Sedge peat
You may need to create a planting pocket from sedge peat if your pomegranate tree does not have a stable bonsai pad. It is also useful as a planting medium for the moss.

Constructing the landscape

A custom-made ceramic tray will give your landscape the best appearance. However, with a large, flat tray such as this, don't be surprised if it is slightly warped. This will add to its charm and character. Make sure it is waterproof to avoid water stains on your furniture.

1 Wash and dry the tray. Arrange the lace rocks to create a pleasing natural landscape that will replicate an eroded cliff face. Position a rock with a steep angle to the left of the landscape to act as the cliff face. Arrange the other rocks to the right so they form a gentle slope. Leave a space between the rocks where the main pomegranate will be. Ensure that the rock with the indentation for the pond is at the correct angle so that it will hold as much water as possible. Position it to the right of the landscape, then line the indentation with pond liner. Holes and crevices in the rocks are mysterious and will add a great deal of beauty to your finished scene, so avoid covering them.

2 When you are satisfied with the arrangement, mark the positions where the three pieces of lace rock should be placed. Glue the rocks with silicone and allow at least 2 hours for the silicone to set.

◀ Silicone glue

One of the benefits of using silicone glue is that you can reposition items simply by lifting the adhesive with a knife. You can buy silicone glue at most art supply stores.

▶ Bonsai wire

Before being planted in the landscape, the fig tree has been trained with wire in semicascade style so that it will hang over the water-filled rock.

▶ Ericaceous soil

Use this soil in the areas around the pond where the rhododendrons will be planted.

Grafting wax

This wax is available from garden centers. You will need it to seal pruning cuts in order to prevent water from entering and rotting the wood. It also cosmetically mask the cuts.

▶ Chick grit

Chick grit is useful as coarse drainage. It is available at farm and feed supply stores.

Pond liner

This is a thick plastic sheeting that does not deteriorate in water. You can buy it at garden centers.

Planting plan

The first tree to plant is the big pomegranate, with a freestanding bonsai pad. Dust a little coarse grit in the bottom of the tray and place the pomegranate on top. Build planting pockets to the left and right with sedge peat (see page 14). Put ericaceous soil in the pocket to the left of the pomegranate and plant the miniature rhododendron. Plant the conifers at the far left of the scene.

In the middle of the planting, build up some sedge peat to about half the height of the rock in the center. Position the semicascade fig tree so it leans toward the pond. Where there is a space between the fig and the middle rock, plant selaginella to add color and contrast. I planted more selaginella further down, by the water, to add color and soften the pond's edge.

Plant the club rush plant behind the fig and the selaginella to create an illusion of water splashing and to lift the background of the scene, then plant the wild fern beside it. Fill planting pockets with ericaceous soil and plant the remaining rhododendrons around the banks of the pond. Plant the 'Nana' pomegranate at the far right toward the back. Fill all spaces with sedge peat, and use moss and chick grit to cover exposed areas of soil.

1. *Punica granatum*
2. *Isolepis cernua*
3. *Ficus cordata* subsp. *salicifolia*
4. *Rhododendron impeditum*
5. *Punica granatum* 'Nana'
6. *Selaginella kraussiana*
7. Wild fern
8. Moss
9. *Cupressus macrocarpa* 'Goldcrest'

CARE

- **Positioning:** The landscape needs sunshine in a cool indoor environment with moist air, such as the windowsill of an unheated lobby or covered porch.
- **Watering:** Pomegranates need a lot of water when in flower. Overhead spraying at night is best as it avoids scorching the leaves. Watch for changes in the soil-mix color—dark soil mix is wet; light is dry. When not in flower, allow the soil to dry out between waterings to ensure good air circulation around the roots.
- **Feeding:** Insert pellets of organic bonsai fertilizer monthly from April to October.
- **Pruning:** Pomegranates tend to make leggy new growth. On alternate years, when the tree develops five leaves, cut back to two. You will lose flowers this way, so allow the tree to grow for a year, followed by severe pruning the following year. For the fig, allow three to five leaves to develop, then cut back to two leaves.

the scenery

▼Moss

I harvest moss from parking lots and sidewalks. It is easiest to collect when it is dry because you can simply lift it off the growing surface. Store dry moss layered in containers to use as needed. When you spray moss with rainwater, it quickly rehydrates and becomes fluffy and a rich green. If you want to glue moss onto rocks, always use it dry.

Selaginella kraussiana

This is a mosslike fern that can grow very quickly and overpower the landscape. To avoid this, break off pieces from the parent plant. Selaginella makes a good alternative to moss as ground cover because it is thicker and denser in structure. In this landscape, I have used it to enhance the rocks and act as an extension to them. Selaginella prefers moist soil. You will need six clumps in this landscape.

▼*Ficus cordata* subsp. *salicifolia*

The fig is ideal to grow indoors, as it tolerates neglect, poor light, and bad watering. This variety needs to be clipped regularly, otherwise the leaves closest to the trunk will begin to yellow in colder weather. The single tree in this landscape is 8 years old. Before being placed in the landscape, it had been trained in semicascade style (see page 111).

◄*Cupressus macrocarpa* 'Goldcrest'

These fresh-green conifers add brightness to the landscape. They are tied with wire to link them into a group, and the top of the foliage has been clipped in the broom style (see page 45). You will need five plants for this landscape.

Literati style

Based on the impressionistic paintings created by the elite artists and scholars of Chinese and Japanese society, the literati is the most expressive and artistic of all bonsai styles and the most challenging to create successfully. The trunk, with its subtle twists and bends, is the primary area of interest. The only rule in creating this style is that it should be 60 to 80 percent bare. Trees with thin trunks such as juniper and pine, are particularly suitable. The pots should be plain and unobtrusive and are usually round.

TIP

When choosing a tree, think of the prints of Horishige and Hokusai, many of which show trees in the literati style. Look for a young nursery pomegranate. Pay particular attention to the trunk, which should have free-flowing curves and unusual or dramatic twists.

❶ Select which side will be the front of the tree. Start with the lowest branches and prune all on the lower two thirds of the trunk. Then prune most of the branches on the upper third of the trunk, leaving only those you think are the most aesthetically pleasing to the whole. Seal the pruning cuts with grafting wax.

❷ Before wiring, carefully consider the trunk and decide whether you want to emphasize any natural curves or create new ones. For maximum trunk support, make sure the wire is placed on the outer apex of the curve of the trunk. Thin out the remaining foliage and wire the branches downward.

❸ Comb and prune the roots into a shallow root system and place the tree in its pot in a considered position. Tweak the tips of the branches. You may change your mind about what should be the front. Keep an open mind, remembering that, in high art, the subject often takes over and points the best way forward.

❹ Leave the wire for a year, removing any shoots that grow on the trunk and any downward shoots in the top third. Finger-prune upward shoots in the top third, holding the branch in one hand and plucking foliage with the other.

▼ *Rhododendron impeditum*

To give the landscape plenty of color in spring, I have used dwarf rhododendrons grown from cuttings. *R. impeditum* has mauve flowers and my cuttings are now 5 years old. You will need four cuttings.

▼ *Isolepis cernua*

There is a single club rush plant in this landscape. The leaves of club rush grow erect and then bend over. Club rush likes moist conditions and humid air, but it will tolerate dryness if you mist it from above. It prefers shade, but I tend to treat the requirements of the larger specimens in the landscape first. This might not always suit the grass, but I make sure the club rush's roots are wet.

▶ *Punica granatum*

The beautifully *neijikan* (meaning "twisted" in Japanese) pomegranate in the landscape is 50 years old. In late summer it has lovely orange flowers. However, I have used this single tree mainly for the beauty of its aged and twisted form and the drama it creates in the landscape. You can train a pomegranate from 2 or 3 years old. Wire the new growth with light-gauge bonsai wire, making S-shaped bends to foreshorten the growth.

Wild fern

The single fern in this landscape seeded itself. Ferns need moist soil and an undisturbed surface to thrive. You can buy ferns from garden centers—try *Polystichum tsus-simense*, which would also suit this landscape.

Punica granatum 'Nana'

For instant, reliable summer color, I have used one 10-year-old pomegranate, as its lovely orange flowers appear without fail every year. You can wire this pomegranate in the twin-trunk style (see page 87).

龍樹龜水

Long Shu Gui Shui

DRAGON TREE
TORTOISE POND

石步天

Shi Bu Tian
STONE STEPS TO HEAVEN

Three rugged mountainous rocks in a stepped formation reach up to heaven in this spectacular landscape. For the Chinese, luck resides in heaven, so by creating this landscape we are lifting our spirits closer to our dreams. In China, a planting such as this would be presented as a gift to an elderly person as a symbol of longevity.

Fiery outbursts of red-stemmed oxalis (*Oxalis vulcanicola* 'Sunset Velvet') and false cypresses (*Chamaecyparis thyoides* 'Andelyensis') lead you toward the three slopes, whose sun-baked steps are adorned with miniature spruces (*Picea abies* 'Little Gem'). Dripping from the sides of the mountains are clusters of the dainty blue alpine, *Sedum hispanicum*. The landscape looks especially beautiful when the early morning sun bathes the steps—it has a heavenly appearance.

This is a large landscape—the tallest mountain is approximately 32 inches (80cm) high—and makes a stunning display. I have created the rocks from ciment fondu and chicken wire built upon sturdy metal supports. The landscape is set in a large, handmade ceramic tray, and gravel around the base of the rocks is used to give the effect of flowing water.

setting up

▲Tray
You will need a shallow water tray approximately 12 by 36 inches (30 by 90cm). For the best appearance, commission a handmade ceramic tray from a potter.

▶Chicken wire
From ¼-inch (5mm) gauge chicken wire, cut one square in each of the following sizes: 40 inches (100cm), 24 inches (60cm) and 16 inches (40cm). These will form the bases onto which fiberglass cloth and ciment fondu will be added to form the rocks.

Protective clothing
Always wear protective gloves when working with fiberglass cloth and a face mask when using cement.

▼Coarse gravel
In this landscape, gravel is used instead of water to represent a flowing river. Its warm tones and contrasting texture against the plants and rocks make the gravel visually pleasing.

Mixing bowl
A glass, 5-inch (12.5cm) mixing bowl is the most suitable for mixing ciment fondu, as it is simple to clean and you can check the water level easily.

Fiberglass cloth
Cut the cloth into twenty 2-inch (5cm) squares, then into triangles. Cutting off-grain makes the cloth stretchy. It is available from craft and art supply stores.

Plastic sheeting
Use this to protect your work surface and to cover the ciment-fondu construction. I sometimes use split-open trash-can liners.

Wire cutters and scissors
You will need wire cutters to cut the chicken wire, and scissors to cut the fiberglass cloth.

Constructing the landscape

Take your time to create the three rocks for the landscape, as they need to appear as realistic as possible. Wear protective gloves when working with the chicken wire and a face mask when mixing and applying the ciment fondu.

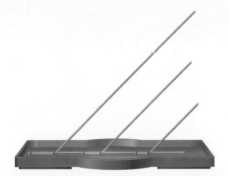

1 Bend 2 inches (5cm) at one end of the longest metal support so that it forms a 45-degree angle. Affix the 2-inch (5cm) section to the tray using quick-drying cement. In the same way, bend 1½ inches (4cm) of the medium-sized support and 1 inch (2.5cm) of the shortest support and secure them both to the tray. Let set.

2 Pleat each of the three chicken-wire squares. Place the largest pleated square onto the longest metal support, overlapping the top and bottom of the support and fanning the wire over the bent metal base. If necessary, cut into some parts of the wire to help you form it and to give the rock a realistic edge. Repeat this process with the medium-sized square of chicken wire and the medium-sized support, and for the smallest sizes of wire and support. When you are happy with the shapes, sew fiberglass cloth to the chicken wire.

3 In a bowl, mix the ciment fondu to the consistency of light cream and apply it to the fiberglass cloth with a paintbrush. You may find this takes several sessions to complete. Whenever you leave the structure, remember to cover it with wet newspaper and a sheet of plastic to prevent it from cracking while drying. The ciment fondu will take 24 hours to set.

▼ Quick-drying cement
Use quick-drying cement to attach the metal supports to the water tray.

Bonsai wire
When two trees are placed close together in the landscape, link them with wire to secure them in position.

Metal supports
Any type of strong, 2-inch-wide (5cm) flat metal will be suitable to support the ciment fondu. You will need three pieces cut to 40 inches (102cm) long, 24 inches (60cm) long, and 16 inches (40cm) long.

▲ Paintbrush
Apply the ciment fondu with a 1-inch-wide (2.5cm) decorator's paintbrush.

Needle and thread
Use strong needle and thread to attach the fiberglass cloth to the chicken wire.

Florist's wire
Bend short lengths of green florist's wire into hairpin shapes and use them to secure moss to the surface of the soil.

▼ Sedge peat
When planting trees clasped to rocks, sedge peat is an ideal medium. Alternatively, use a sticky mixture of half peat and half clay blended with water. The mixture helps the roots stick to the rock and will harden after 12 hours or so.

▶ Ciment fondu
A natural, rocklike appearance can be achieved by using ciment fondu.

Bonsai soil mix
Use this for planting and for mixing with sedge peat to make planting pockets on the slopes of the rock.

Newspaper
Use sheets of newspaper that have been soaked in water to cover the ciment-fondu rock while it sets. Wrap plastic sheeting around the newspaper to prevent it drying.

Planting plan

Plant the spruce trees on the slopes, decreasing their number as you go higher. The trees should also point slightly downward as they ascend. In nature, trees are denser and thicker on sheltered slopes, so use taller trees with a thicker girth on the lower slopes and shorter, thinner trees higher up. Use groups of trees to give the appearance of one tree with a thick girth on the lowest parts of the landscape. This will add to the illusion of height and naturalness. I planted five trees at the top, six in the center front, eight at the back, and three on the small middle rock. Create sedge-peat planting pockets (see page 14), and position them along the rocks. Place the spruces in the planting pockets and cover the roots with bonsai soil mix. When you use more than two trees together, join them with bonsai wire to make planting easier.

Plant the prepared oxalis at the center base of the landscape in bonsai soil mix and sedge peat. Plant two false cypress at the foot of the rock on the left-hand side, and one toward the back on the right. Make planting pockets on the lower edges of the sides of the rocks, and plant the sedum so they gently spill over. Cover excess roots with moss speared with florist's wire. Plant the lady's mantle at the base of the rocks at the back and front of the landscape. Scatter coarse gravel over the base of the tray. Trim excess growth at the base of the landscape to reveal some rock.

1. *Sedum hispanicum*
2. *Chamaecyparis thyoides* 'Andelyensis'
3. *Oxalis vulcanicola* 'Sunset Velvet'
4. *Alchemilla ellenbeckii*
5. Moss
6. *Picea abies* 'Little Gem'

CARE

- **Positioning:** Place the landscape outdoors. Allow for about 2 hours of sunshine, with the remainder of the day in the shade.
- **Watering:** At least twice a day, morning and evening, water the landscape using a fine rose-spray head. Rock plantings tend to dry out quickly, so always keep them well watered.
- **Feeding:** Feed once a month with liquid organic fertilizer, such as natural seaweed feed Maxicrop, and twice a month during the growing season.
- **Pruning:** Prune with sharp scissors to maintain a tight silhouette. Thin out the foliage on the inside and underside of the trees.

---

the scenery

▼ *Oxalis vulcanicola* 'Sunset Velvet'

This is an easy plant to grow, and its lovely gold-red leaves and stems make an attractive contrast to the fresh greens in the planting. Take cuttings in spring and summer. Cut a 2-inch (5cm) stem from the parent plant and remove the two lowest leaves. Insert it in a small pot of moist soil mix. When the plant is 1 year old, prepare a bonsai pad (see page 14). Six plants are needed here.

▶ *Picea abies* 'Little Gem'

I chose this spruce for its fine foliage and blue color, which echoes the sky. The foliage can simply be trimmed with scissors to achieve the correct shape. Remove all foliage from beneath the branches and any unnecessary growth toward the trunk, as this will brown and die off. You will need twenty-two 6-year-old trees for this landscape. Prepare bonsai pads to make planting on the rock easier (see page 14).

▼ *Alchemilla ellenbeckii*

I have used this miniature lady's mantle to contrast with the oxalis and false cypress. It has tiny greenish flowers in summer. You will need two plants for this landscape.

Root on rock

Technically difficult to achieve, my root-on-rock style is a more advanced version of root-clasped-to-rock (see page 27) and takes from 4 to 10 years to create. The Trident maple is one of the best, most vigorous species and is good for beginners. White pine is ideal, but takes much longer. You can also use juniper, spruce (as here), larch, and cotoneaster. Cuttings are best to use for propagation.

1 ▶ Having rooted your spruce cutting, plant it in a very deep pot with slatted sides in deep, rich soil and leave for 1 year to allow the roots to get long enough to arrange over your rock.

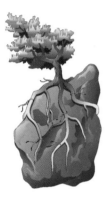

2 Comb the roots and drape over the vertical rock. Don't choose a rock so beautiful it would be a distraction. The aim is for a unified whole among tree, roots, and rock in the finished plant. Making sure the tips of the roots are facing straight down, lightly glue with epoxy glue, and tie with very fine bonsai wire.

3 Plant in rich soil in a very deep training pot with drainage holes at least ½ inch (12mm) in diameter, double-checking the roots are facing straight down. Leave for 5 to 6 years undisturbed. You can check once a year but be careful not to disturb the tree or move it in any way.

4 While the tree is still in the deep pot, trim the upper branches to balance it. When you can see the roots have firmly clasped the rock, remove the wire and replant the tree in a shallow training pot. After the tree has settled, begin to shape the upper branches.

5 Slowly expose the roots over a period of years by gently dusting away the soil from the top surface. As the top part of the root is exposed to sunlight it will become thicker and gnarled, while the lower roots will grow down into the soil.

▼ Sedum hispanicum

This blue alpine echoes the blue of the *Picea abies* 'Little Gem.' Approximately six clumps are positioned in the landscape so that they hang gently over the sides of the slopes.

▶ Chamaecyparis thyoides 'Andelyensis'

This false cypress has dark green foliage that turns yellow and reddish bronze in full sun. I chose this plant because it complements the red foliage of the oxalis and seems to reflect the brilliance of the sun. This variety has exceptionally fine foliage, giving the landscape a light and fresh appearance in contrast to the rugged rocks. You will need three 4-year-old plants with bonsai pads (see page 14) for this landscape.

▼ Moss

Attach dry or wet moss to wet quick-drying cement to add to the natural appearance of the rocks.

Shi Bu Tian
STONE STEPS
TO HEAVEN

SPRUCE
AT A GLANCE

🌿 False cypress is an evergreen conifer found mainly in mountainous areas of the northern hemisphere.

🌿 *P. orientalis* 'Gracilis,' *P. abies* 'Nidiformis,' *P. abies* 'Pygmea,' *P. glauca* 'Echiniformis,' and *P. glauca* 'Albertinana Conica' are all good for bonsai. The Sakhalin spruce, *P. glehnii* (sometimes wrongly referred to as *P. Jezoenis* or ezo spruce), is most commonly used for bonsai. Suitable for all styles except broom style, this spruce is particularly useful in group plantings and is ideal for rock styles (see pages 27, 57, and 105). Usually it's shown in unglazed, dark-colored pots or, for groups, on slabs of slate.

🌿 Spruces like sandy compost and not too much water. They love full sun throughout the year but like some shade in very hot sun.

Deng Hua
LANTERN FLOWERS

Here is a grand and graceful planting that reminds me of a mature woman. At the height of summer, when yang—the masculine influence—is at its strongest, she surprises the viewer with a display of beautiful, vividly colored lanterns—a token of the feminine yin. The lantern is a symbol of illumination and knowledge, and the fuchsia (*Fuchsia procumbens* 'Rose of Castile')—or hua flower—is associated with a beautiful woman who is herself a flower reborn. I have added two tiny lanterns to reflect the floral lanterns and draw the eye deeper into the landscape.

I have been tending this fuchsia for 20 years, and early each spring, as it begins to make new growth, I decide how to trim the little tree. Sometimes I leave the growth and remove only the leaves. This reveals the amazing red stems that carry the beautiful flowers. Fuchsia is a native of South America and loves living in my cool conservatory, where it is reluctant to shed the previous year's leaves.

I use two water trays in this landscape. One holds the fuchsia in a wooden tub that is cleverly clothed in artificial rock made from chicken wire, fiberglass cloth, and ciment fondu. The other tray holds a planting of grasses and oxalis (*Oxalis vulcanicola* 'Sunset Velvet') whose forms complement the rock and fuchsia perfectly.

setting up

▼ Trays
I have used two Italian, handmade circular trays. Each one measures 15 inches (38cm) in diameter. These will create an image of two stepping-stones: one containing the rock and the other a freely growing and untamed planting.

Aluminum gauze
Boulders to mask the edges of the pot and tub are formed from ten 3-inch (7.5cm) squares of aluminum gauze.

Needle and thread
Use a large needle and strong sewing thread to sew the fiberglass cloth to the chicken-wire before molding.

◀ Chicken wire
Use fine-gauge, ½-inch (1cm) chicken wire to form the rock. You will need two pieces of chicken wire 12 inches (30cm) square.

Paintbrushes
Use a medium-sized paint brush to apply the ceramic paint to the trays, and a thick brush to apply the ciment fondu to the wooden tub.

▲ Florist's wire
Bent florist's wire is used to attach the rock and the boulders to the tub.

◀ Protective clothing
Always wear protective gloves when working with fiberglass cloth, and a face mask when using cement.

▶ Wire cutters
Use wire cutters to cut the chicken wire.

Fiberglass cloth
You will need fiberglass cloth to attach to the chicken wire before molding.

Constructing the landscape

Start by making a sketch of your finished rocks. Spread a piece of plastic sheeting on your work surface. Wear protective gloves when working with the chicken wire and a face mask when mixing and applying the ciment fondu.

1 The fuschia pot is housed in a baseless marine-plywood tub hidden under the ciment-fondu rock. For the sides of the tub you will need two pieces of marine plywood 8 by 16 inches (20 by 40cm) and two pieces 6 by 16 inches (15 by 40cm). For the corner posts you will need four 16-inch (40cm) lengths of 1 by 1 inch (2.5 by 2.5cm) plywood. Nail or staple the side pieces lengthwise to the posts. The tub must be at least as deep as the pot and narrow enough that the lip of the pot is supported by the tub's edges.

2 Cut two 12-inch (30cm) chicken wire squares, and sew fiberglass cloth onto them on both sides. Pleat the squares into fan shapes, then pull them out and mold them to look like rock (see pages 12–13). Using florist's wire or staples, attach the rock shapes to the plywood tub, leaving space for the cascading plant (check by positioning the plant). Once the rock is the correct shape, coat it and the tub with ciment fondu, then wrap them in damp newspaper and plastic, and let dry for 24 hours. Then rinse the rock.

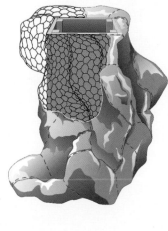

3 Apply two coats of paint to the trays, and let dry. You must also make small boulders using 3-inch (7.5cm) aluminum gauze squares and plaster gauze (see page 13). Pleat the aluminum, then form it into boulder shapes by fanning out some areas and pressing into others. Cover with wet plaster gauze, then sprinkle with some quick-drying cement and sand mixture. Leave the boulders for a day to set. They will be used to mask the edges of the tub and pot (see page 110). Once the ciment fondu rock and tub are dry, cement them onto a tray. Then lower in your potted fuchsia.

Quick-drying cement and builder's sand
Make a 50:50 mixture of quick-drying cement and builder's sand to give a sandstone effect to the boulders you will form out of plaster gauze. You will also need quick-drying cement to attach the rock to the tray.

◀ Silicone glue
You will need silicone glue to attach the moss and handmade boulders. Silicone glue is a useful waterproof adhesive that can be easily removed by prizing it off with a knife.

▶ Mixing bowls
Use an old plastic bowl or something similar to soak the plaster gauze and a small bowl to mix up the ciment fondu.

Hammer and nails or staple gun
Use ¼-inch (5mm) nails to assemble the wooden tub, or use a staple gun if you prefer.

Marine plywood
You will need marine plywood to create a tub to contain the fuchsia pot. The tub must be at least as deep as the pot; the tub here is 12 inches (30cm) deep, but the depth of your tub will depend on the measurements of your fuchsia's existing pot. The wooden tub will be in a damp environment, so it is important to use marine plywood, which will not rot.

Ceramic paint
Use gray ceramic paint on the trays.

▶ Ciment fondu
Ciment fondu is made especially for underwater applications.

Plaster gauze
Plaster gauze can only be used for making rocks that will be kept indoors, as it is not frost-proof.

Newspaper and a plastic sheet
Use wet newspaper to cover the ciment fondu while it sets, and then wrap it in plastic sheeting to retain moisture.

Planting plan

Place the fuchsia in its pot into the tub you have made. Position it so that the overhang is placed where there is no ciment-fondu rock at the sides of the pot. Glue moss and boulders around the top of the pot and the tub to mask their edges. Place the boulders so that there are flat areas and high areas. You can use pieces of florist's wire as well as glue to keep the boulders in place.

Add interest to the planting by gluing dry moss to some of the exposed areas of ciment fondu. This will also help give the landscape a natural appearance.

Attach the two ceramic lanterns to the viewing side of the rock. Place one almost in the center of the rock and the other at the base. Plant the erodium to the left of the base of the planted tub.

Plant the second tray with the grasses and oxalis, arranging them so the planting is balanced and graceful.

1. *Fuchsia procumbens* 'Rose of Castile'
2. Moss
3. Japanese lantern
4. *Erodium reichardii* 'Roseum'
5. *Oxalis vulcanicola* 'Sunset Velvet'
6. *Isolepis cernua*
7. *Schoenoplectus tabernaemontani*

CARE

- **Positioning:** If possible, place the landscape in a cool greenhouse, or otherwise on a sunny windowsill of a covered porch or vestibule or other unheated room. Be aware that too much fluctuation in temperature will not be beneficial for the planting.
- **Watering:** Water every day from spring to autumn. Use rainwater or bottled water, as tap water causes lime deposits to build up around the trunk of the plant and the rim of the pots. Spray the foliage mornings and evenings on sunny days.
- **Feeding:** As fuchsia is a hungry plant, feed it once a week with bonsai fertilizer, following the manufacturer's instructions.
- **Pruning:** In spring, when new growth begins to appear on the fuchsia, start to prune according to the clip-and-grow method (see page 75).

the scenery

◀ *Schoenoplectus tabernaemontani*
This erect grass is a weed in many gardens. I have used one plant to exaggerate the linear formation of the wild planting next to the fuchsia. It gives an exciting lift, like fireworks, to the heavy rock beside it.

Japanese lanterns
To give the design a rustic feel, I have added two handmade ceramic lanterns.

▼ *Fuchsia procumbens* 'Rose of Castile'
This is a trailing fuchsia. The photograph below shows a cutting I have recently taken from the parent plant. The main trunk is about 6 years old and it is ready to be used in a landscape. Old-wood cuttings can be taken from plants of this age. The single plant in the landscape is 20 years old and has been growing in a tall bonsai pot. As I did not want to disturb its roots, I made a wooden tub in which to place the existing pot.

▼ *Erodium reichardii* 'Roseum'
The leaves and flowers of this dainty plant are similar to those of a water lily. I have planted a single erodium at the base of the rock so that the plant's delicate form contrasts against the strong shape of the stone. Its flowers also add brightness here, and the planting looks like water flowing past the base of the rock.

Semicascade style

Sometimes referred to as the "looking over water" style, any bonsai with a horizontal or near-horizontal trunk will qualify as a semicascade. Apart from the uprights, any tree can be grown in this style, but it is particularly suited to cedars, junipers, cherries, willows, and many of the flowering plants such as chrysanthemums, star jasmine, and fuchsia.

TIP

When training a tree or plant in semicascade style, keep in mind the image of a tree hanging over the edge of a cliff or waterfall. In this natural situation, a tree will at first struggle upward, in the direction of the sun, but will eventually be bent back by the harsh mountain weather.

❶ Choose a deep pot for stability and plant the tree before you begin shaping. Unlike with other styles, position the tree in the center of the pot. Plant so that it leans slightly, in order to encourage the development of the cascade.

❷ Taking the cascading branches for the front of the tree, begin to shape it. For internal as well as external consistency, make sure everything leans in the same direction—the branches, the trunk, and the tip of the apex (if there is one; this style does not have to have an apex).

❸ The wiring of the branches is crucial, as the shape of the bending branches is the most important feature of this style. The trunk and branches must first lean away from the direction of the cascade, to indicate the tree's natural growth, and then bend over to begin the cascade.

❹ The branches should project over the rim of the container but reach no lower than its base. You can train those at the back of the tree closer to the trunk than you would do in other styles.

▼ *Isolepis cernua*

This magical grass, known as club rush, has been used twice in the freely planted tray to contrast with the fuchsia-planted rock. The grass has a pleasing growth habit: The stems initially grow erect, but later they curve softly and have tiny, ball-shaped flowers at the tips. This grass prefers some shade and moist soil.

▶ *Oxalis vulcanicola* '**Sunset Velvet**'

Greenish-yellow leaves eventually turn red on this oxalis. The leaves and red stems work well with the club rush in the freely planted tray. Oxalis likes a damp soil mix. You can take 2-inch (5cm) cuttings in late spring and early summer. Remove the two lowest leaves and push the cuttings into sand, either in a small pot or in a cold frame. Keep the cuttings moist; they will root in a couple of weeks. You will need four plants here.

▶ **Moss**

You can use pieces of dried found moss, or buy dried moss from garden centers. Glue a little dry moss to the rock to give it a natural appearance.

Deng Hua
LANTERN
FLOWERS

FUCHSIA
AT A GLANCE

Fuchsia is a subtropical plant, native to South and Central America. There are thousands of fuchsia hybrids, many of which can be used for bonsai. The most successful are the small-flowered varieties—*Fuchsia microphylla* 'Tom Thumb' and 'Lady Thumb.' The hardiest and best fuchsias for bonsai are from the *Fuchsia magellanica* species. The weaker variegated forms are best avoided.

Fuchsia can be grown in informal upright, cascade, semicascade, slanting, and rock styles. Treelike forms, or standards, can be created by tying the stem to a cane and rubbing off the side shoots to make a trunk.

This plant is simple to maintain and easy to propagate by cuttings. Keep it in a basic soil mix in full sun. Water daily during the growing season. Repot annually in spring.

飛
龍

Fei Long
FLYING DRAGON

For many people, the wizened trunk and spiky foliage tufts of the Japanese larch *(Larix kaempferi)* epitomize the traditional Japanese landscape seen so often in prints by the masters. I have used the larch to represent a dragon flying over the heavens. In Chinese philosophy, flying is an aspect of yin—the feminine force—whereas a dragon is an aspect of yang—the masculine. The seed of a wild larch may be blown onto a mountain precipice, where it germinates and thrives, so I feel this landscape is a good pictorial representation of a mythical flying dragon.

This landscape represents a weatherworn rock on a mountainside. It is similar to the harsh environment where a bonsai grower found this larch many years ago. The tiny larch seed had fought against the elements and was growing strongly, its roots firmly anchored inside a crevice. Every twist and turn of its gnarled trunk was testimony to its struggle for survival. I took over the care of this 50-year-old tree 20 years ago.

Fei Long sits on a grand slab of blue-gray slate. At the left of the landscape, a little figure of a Chinese man can be seen beneath an overhang of rock covered in saxifrage *(Saxifraga cochlearis)*.

setting up

Stone slab or slate
You will need a large piece of natural stone slab or slate measuring 12 by 20 inches (30 by 50cm) and ½ inch (1cm) thick.

◄ Ciment fondu in white and gray
White ciment fondu is first added to the rock pot, then gray is added. I left a few white patches to give a sharp look to the edge of the pot.

Chicken wire
Use ½-inch (1cm) gauge chicken wire to form a double-layered, half-crescent-shaped rock pot. The double layer reinforces the base and adds to the aesthetic appeal of the pot.

◄ Florist's wire
Bend short lengths of green florist's wire into hairpin shapes to secure the plants to the rock pot.

Staple gun
Use this to attach the chicken wire to the wooden base.

Wooden base
To support the ciment-fondu rock pot, you will need a piece of wood 6 by 10 inches (15 by 25cm) and ¼ inch (5mm) thick with a 1- by 2-inch (2.5 by 5cm) drainage hole cut in the bottom.

◄ Raffia
You may need this to secure your Japanese larch to the pot.

Newspaper
Use wet sheets of newspaper to cover the ciment-fondu rock while it sets. Wrap plastic sheeting around the newspaper to prevent it from drying out.

Plastic sheeting
Use this to protect your work surface while working with ciment fondu and to wrap around the structure while it sets.

▼ Chick grit
Throw chick grit over the wet ciment fondu, and add it to the planting to give the appearance of poor, stony soil.

Constructing the landscape

Look out for pictures of curved and undulating mountains that could be a reference for your half-crescent rock pot. Note their twists and turns and how the weather has affected their surfaces. Wear protective gloves when working with the chicken wire and a face mask when mixing and applying the ciment fondu.

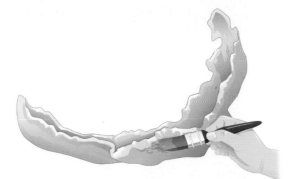

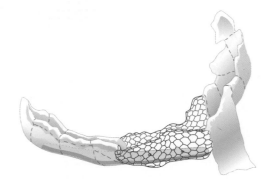

1 To make the hollow half-crescent pot, cut an 18-inch (45cm) chicken wire square and stitch fiberglass cloth to it (see page 12). Now cut another wire square in the same way for the top layer of the rock. Stitch a square of fiberglass cloth to one side of the wire; the cloth side will face upward. Pleat both layers of wired cloth at ½-inch (1cm) intervals. Fan them out into half-moon shapes, molding uneven indentations and crevices. Cut away the excess if you have any unattractive bunched-up areas. Staple the first piece to the wooden base and continue to shape it. Place the second piece at a slight angle over the first to create interesting gaps. Create a dip in the center for the larch.

2 Using scissors and wire cutters, cut a drainage hole to match the hole in the wooden base. In a bowl, prepare a white ciment-fondu mixture and use a paintbrush to cover the entire wired-cloth structure with it. Cover with wet newspaper and a plastic sheet and let set for 24 hours (see pages 12–13). Mix up the gray ciment fondu and apply it to the structure, leaving some small areas of white ciment fondu exposed to act as reflection from the sun.

3 Throw handfuls of chick grit over the wet ciment fondu to create texture. Allow to set for 24 hours.

◄Wire cutters and scissors
You will need wire cutters and scissors to cut the wired cloth.

Fiberglass cloth
Cut three squares of fiberglass cloth 18 by 18 inches (45 by 45cm).

►Mixing bowl
Use a bowl to mix up the ciment fondu. A glass bowl is preferable, as you can monitor the water level easily.

◄Sedge peat
This makes a good planting pocket for the sempervivum at the base of the rock.

Needle and thread
Use a strong needle and thread to sew the fiberglass cloth onto the chicken wire.

Plastic netting
This acts as a drainage medium.

▼Paintbrush
A 1½-inch (4cm) decorator's brush is ideal for applying the ciment fondu.

►Protective clothing
Always wear protective gloves when working with fiberglass cloth and a face mask when using cement.

Akadama
This acts as a drainage medium. Sift the akadama into coarse, medium, and fine grades (see page 9).

Planting plan

Place plastic netting over the drainage hole. Add akadama to the bottom of the rock pot, using the coarser grade first, then adding the medium grade, and finally applying the finest grade. If you have a good, firm bonsai pad on your Japanese larch, it can be placed directly into the rock pot. If the pad is not very strong and stable, use raffia to tie the tree to the rock pot. Add more medium-grade akadama to just cover the bonsai pad. Finally, add fine akadama, dusting it over the surface of the planting.

Plant the saxifrage at the right-hand base of the tree. Try not to cover the roots of the larch, as they will grow attractively gnarled with time. Below the saxifrage, plant the mint using U-shaped florist's wire to hold it in place, if necessary.

Place the entire planting on the stone slab or slate. Make a sausage from sedge peat to contain the sempervivum. Position a sedge-peat sausage to the left-hand side of the landscape. Add a thin layer of medium-grade akadama and place the figurine on the outside edge of the akadama so that it covers the feet. Plant the sempervivum in planting pockets of sedge peat, positioning the rosettes to lean slightly toward the viewer. Finally, add a sprinkling here and there of chick grit to give the growing surface an arid appearance.

1. *Larix kaempferi*
2. *Saxifraga cochlearis*
3. *Sempervivum tectorum*
4. *Mentha requienii*
5. Figurine

CARE

- **Positioning:** Place the landscape outdoors. Larches like a spell of frost, plenty of sunshine, and fresh air.
- **Watering:** From spring until mid-fall, water every day and twice during hot spells, using a fine rose-spray head.
- **Feeding:** Once a month from spring to mid-fall, feed the landscape with an organic fertilizer, such as Maxicrop.
- **Pruning:** Prune the branches from mid- to late summer. New growth can be pinched out from early summer onward. Allow new shoots to elongate when buds appear, then train them to an outward position with wire.

---

the scenery

▼ *Mentha requienii*

This tiny, purple-flowered mint provides a soft textural change in contrast to the fleshy leaves of the sempervivum above it. The mint flowers toward the end of spring. You will need one plant for the landscape.

▶ *Sempervivum tectorum*

I have used this sempervivum to create a focal point of the figure at the foot of the rock. This alpine forms delightful hummocks of green and crimson, giving a bright touch of color to the scene in winter.

▶ Figurine

I have added a little Chinese figurine at the base of the landscape to give a sense of scale and to introduce life to the scene. I have positioned him to lean over the planting. He could be climbing up the mountainside, or perhaps he is a woodsman resting a while from gathering wood. I find that using figurines and other ornaments can bring a landscape to life and suggest a story to the viewer.

Creating *jin,* or driftwood

In the driftwood style, large sections of the trunk and certain branches are deliberately made to look like bleached driftwood. It is a very dramatic style, with the tree looking remarkably like it has taken a battering from strong winds or heavy snow. The effect can be created artificially by stripping bark and cambium from a live tree, or it can be created from a tree that is already partly dead. The area of driftwood is usually the center of interest, and the entire design of the tree should be carefully built around this feature.

TIP

In traditional bonsai, the peeled branch is usually cut short to create a stumpy *jin,* as you would find in nature after a dead branch has broken off. However, in my landscapes I prefer to preserve the shape of the branch—be creative in how you use these beautiful forms.

1 Prune the lower branches that you want to use to create the *jin,* leaving them as stubs jutting out of the trunk.

2 To loosen the bark and make it ready to peel, grip it with a pair of jinning pliers and lightly crush. Pinch evenly all the way around from different angles.

3 For a natural look on larger branches and the trunk, grip the bark with pliers and gently rip. To add sharper, more dramatic edges to the *jin,* define the branch stubs with a knife.

4 Clean exposed surfaces with a wire brush. Shape immediately. Let dry for 3 months, then treat regularly with lime sulfur. Protect the soil with a cloth, and paint on the lime using a fine artist's brush. This stops the *jin* from rotting. To tone down whiteness, mix the lime with a little india ink.

▼ *Saxifraga cochlearis*

This alpine plant conjures up an arid terrain, as you would expect to see at the top of a mountain. The tight mass of the flowerlike rosettes is particularly attractive clothing the rocky form. I used six plants here. Saxifrage needs well-drained soil, so it is essential to plant with chick grit.

▶ *Larix kaempferi*

The Japanese larch in my landscape is 50 years old, but you can use a well-styled tree that is 3 or 4 years old. The trunk will be slimmer but, if it is well trained, a tree can look quite old at this stage. The tree will need a well-developed bonsai pad (see page 14). Larches grow well from seed. They can be sown from late fall throughout the winter, but late-winter sowings seem to germinate the most successfully. Sow the seeds in freely draining soil mix that is 50:50 grit and coir or peat. When the seedlings are 1 inch (2.5cm) high, feed them with half-strength organic fertilizer.

TIP

Deadwood occurring naturally on a Japanese larch will be very different from the deadwood of another tree. When planning the form your bonsai tree will take, it is always helpful to refer to an example of the same tree growing wild—and try to recreate nature in miniature.

Fe Long
FLYING
DRAGON

SEDUM
AT A GLANCE

✿ These tiny, roselike tufts with fine, white
edges are used for bonsai in a way similar
to that of moss. An Asian alpine from the
Crassulaceae family, sedum grow at very
high altitudes on the edges of mountains.
Bluish-green in color, they reflect the
sky well and prevent soil from washing
away. They are very free draining and are
therefore ideal for rock plantings.

✿ To propagate, take a section and plant it
in a 50:50 mixture of chick grit and bonsai
soil in a flat tray with drainage. When it has
spread into its own bonsai pad, lift it with
a spatula and place it on the soil.

✿ In winter, dust underneath the rosettes with
grit so they don't get waterlogged and
rot at the center.

PLANT DIRECTORY

I chose the plants to use in my landscapes for their particular colors, forms, and growth habits. By selecting trees that can be trained to grow in a way that suits the landscape, you can replicate a natural landscape in miniature. When you choose plants to grow alongside your main trees or as ground cover, think about the effect you wish to create. You can lighten a dark corner with a bright-leaved specimen or create the effect of flowing water with a plant that has tiny leaves. It's fun to experiment with the plants as you gain experience.

Acer palmatum 'Shindeshojo'

This Japanese maple has beautiful scarlet spring growth. If you cannot locate 'Shindeshojo', 'Bloodgood' will work well in its place. 'Shindeshojo' likes rich, moist, well-drained soil. It thrives in full light but needs protection from very hot sun, severe frost, and wind.

Acorus gramineus

Sweet flag is a cultivated bog grass, easily obtained from aquarium stores. The grassy leaves form fan-shaped tufts, which echo the shape of water flowing over rock. It prefers cool, damp conditions and partial shade.

Alchemilla ellenbeckii

This miniature lady's mantle has very attractive red stems, scalloped green foilage, and tiny greenish flowers in summer. Found wild in African marshes and bogs, it likes very moist to boggy sandy soil and partial shade.

Armeria juniperifolia 'Bevan's Variety'

I use this plant to represent tufts of grass, though it bears white flowers in summer. The rich green foliage curls attractively. A hardy plant, it likes free-draining soil or compost and thrives in sun or shade. It needs protection from severe frosts.

Armeria maritima 'Alba'

This white-flowered sea thrift looks very effective growing at the sides of a container—the narrow green leaves curling over the edge give the appearance of long grass growing on a mountainside. It likes free-draining soil in full sun.

Armeria maritima 'Nifty Thrifty'

'Nifty Thrifty' is a seaside alpine with variegated, straplike foliage and striking cherry-pink flowers (which you may want to remove to avoid throwing a landscape off balance). It likes fine, well-drained soil. A hardy plant, it can tolerate most conditions, including strong winds and salty air, but prefers full sun.

Azorella trifurcata

A compact, evergreen perennial from South America, azorella has glossy, deep green foilage with tiny lobed leaves and produces yellow flowers in summer. It is often mistaken for moss and is ideal to use as ground cover in a landscape. This plant likes moist, well-drained soil and full sun.

Bambusa multiplex

As it is invasive in the garden, this bamboo is best grown in a container. You can take cuttings from a parent plant and house them in a glass dish. (Monitor the water level simply by looking through the glass.) It likes humus-rich soil and full sun or dappled shade in warm, damp conditions.

Carex comans 'Frosted Curls'

This evergreen grasslike perennial has silvery green leaves that add movement to a scene and provide contrast to the rock. It likes moist, well-drained soil and prefers full sun or partial shade.

Chamaecyparis pisifera 'Boulevard'

The 'Boulevard' cypress grows into a conical shape and its feathery foliage has a lovely blueish tinge that deepens into purple in winter. Requiring moist, well-drained soil and compost, it likes full sun and needs protection from strong winds.

Chamaecyparis pisifera 'Tsukumo'

The fine, dark green foliage of this cypress means that at just 2 years old it can be used to represent distant mountain pines. It tolerates cool conditions by a well-lit window, but shield it from full sun or the leaves will scorch.

Chamaecyparis thyoides 'Andelyensis'

Better known as Atlantic white cedar, this tree has fine, dark green foliage that turns reddish bronze in full sun. It is hardy in winter but temperamental. It likes full sun (though avoid scorching) and very fast-draining soil that must not dry out.

Cotoneaster congestus

This plant flowers and fruits easily, its red berries resembling miniature apples. You can plant it directly into a landscape as 1-inch (2.5cm) cuttings. Tolerant of most light and soil conditions, *C. congestus* prefers sun but can grow in the shade. Don't let the soil dry out.

Cotoneaster conspicuus

This cotoneaster readily self-sows and grows well from cuttings. A mass of white blossoms in spring are followed in late summer and fall by orange berries. Easy to grow and tolerant of most light and soil conditions, it prefers sun but can grow in shade. Don't let the soil dry out.

Cuppressus macrocarpa 'Goldcrest'

I chose this tree, readily available from garden centers, for its attractive, bright, golden-yellow foliage. It requires a position in full sun and well-drained soil to thrive. You should protect it from wind and frost in winter.

Erodium reichardii 'Roseum'

The leaves and flowers of this dainty plant are similar to those of a water lily. I plant erodium next to rocks, where its delicate form offers an attractive contrast. Its pale pink flowers also add brightness to a scene. It likes gritty soil and full sun.

Euphorbia cyparissias

Cypress spurge has fine, copper-tinged foliage with lime-green flowers in spring. Beware its white milky sap, which can badly irritate the skin; wear gloves when handling it. Euphoribia prefers full sun and does best in poorer garden soil that is moist and well-drained.

Ficus cordata subsp. salicifolia

Ficus cordata subsp. *salicifolia* needs to be clipped regularly, otherwise the leaves closest to the trunk will yellow in colder weather, resulting in leggy growth. The tree is ideal for growing indoors, as it can tolerate neglect, poor light, and bad watering.

Fuchsia microphylla

This fuchsia has very small pink flowers, which are borne on the tips of the foliage pad in summer. I use it to add color and summer interest to a landscape. It needs moist, well-drained soil in sun or partial shade. Do not over water or allow it to dry out. Protect it from frost in winter.

Fuchsia procumbens 'Rose of Castile'

A trailing fuchsia looks good over water or on a mountain. Take softwood cuttings from May to July (autumn hardwood cuttings take longer to root). It requires moist but well-drained soil in sun or partial shade. Do not over water or allow it to dry out, and protect it from frost.

Geranium robertianum

Better known as herb Robert, this plant often grows in wild and waste areas. It has reddish leaves, and pink, star-shaped flowers in summer. It likes full shade with moist to average soil. If grown in moist shade, the leaves will retain their red color through winter.

Isolepis cernua

Also known as club rush, this grass initially grows erect, but later its stems curve and produce tiny, ball-shaped flowers at the tips. A native of wet, mostly coastal areas, it prefers moist soil and some shade.

Juniperus chinensis

A classic tree for bonsai, this plant can be wired into wonderful shapes. It likes dry conditions and full sun. Place it in the shade when the sun is very hot to prevent the foliage from scorching. Water daily in summer; keep the soil moist in winter.

Juniperus chinensis 'Shimpaku'

With its fine, blue-green needles and reddish trunk, this elegant juniper is another classic tree for bonsai. It likes dry conditions and full sun. Place it in the shade in very hot sun to prevent the foliage from scorching. Water daily in summer; keep the soil moist in winter.

Juniperus procumbens 'Nana'

The small needles of this juniper make its foliage appear dense. It is a good tree for rock plantings, as it easily develops foliage pads and tolerates dry conditions. It likes full sun, but place it in shade when the sun is very hot. Water daily in summer; keep the soil moist in winter.

Larix kaempferi

A Japanese larch grows to between 80 and 100 feet (24 and 30m) in its natural habitat but can be tamed by root and branch pruning to suit a bonsai landscape. It prefers full sun and moist, well-drained, slightly acidic to neutral soil, but it can also tolerate poorly drained soil.

Leptinella squalida

A delicate evergreen alpine from New Zealand, this plant resembles a miniature fern. In spring, tufts of green new growth break through the reddish brown winter foliage. It has a creeping habit that makes it a useful alternative to moss. It prefers full sun and can tolerate poor soil.

Lonicera nitida 'Baggesen's Gold'

This delicate, gold-colored boxleaf honeysuckle is easy to grow. The stems will root almost immediately, and if you clip it to almost any shape it will bounce back with new growth. It is not fussy about soil, as long as it is moist and well drained. It prefers full sun or partial shade.

Lunularia cruciata

Better known as crescent-cup liverwort, this plant is commonly found in damp parts of the garden. Its tiny bright green leaves contrast nicely with moss. Position it next to a pool in a bonsai landscape to echo its natural habitat. It grows in moist conditions in soil or on rocks.

Malus toringoides

This variety of crab apple originated in China. It has small, alternate, narrow-toothed leaves and white flowers that are followed by yellow berries in fall. A very hardy plant, it is easy to grow and does best outdoors, as it needs lots of fresh air and full sun.

Malus x zumi 'Golden Hornet'

'Golden Hornet' crab apple bears pinkish, roselike flowers in spring and yellow fruits in fall. The crab apples usually stay on after the leaves have dropped, which is very attractive. It will grow in any position and in average soil but particularly likes chalky soil.

Mentha requienii

Also called Corsican mint, this tiny, purple-flowered mint creeps along the ground and gives a soft texture to a landscape. It flowers toward the end of spring and into early summer and likes shade and moist soil.

Oxalis vulcanicola 'Sunset Velvet'

This golden sorrel is a newly available cultivar that reminds me of the warmth of the setting sun. Ideal for brightening dark niches among rocks, it sports tiny yellow flowers in summer. It prefers moist soil of any type and can grow in full shade but prefers partial shade.

Phyllostachys aureosulcata 'Spectabilis'

Very attractive with orange-yellow stems, this bamboo is not too large to be tamed. Its internodes are marked at alternate intervals. In spring and summer, overhead spray twice a day, morning and evening. It likes moist, well-drained soil.

Picea abies 'Little Gem'

I chose this spruce for its fine foliage and striking blue color, which echoes the sky. The foliage can be trimmed with scissors to achieve the correct shape. It tolerates a range of well-drained soils and climates.

Pilea microphylla

Pilea is a fairly unusual plant; if you can't find it, *Selaginella kraussiana* also works well. The clippings will root readily in a water tray, ensuring you have a supply for your landscapes. Pilea prefers well-drained ordinary garden soil in partial shade or partial sun.

Pleioblastus gramineus

A Japanese bamboo with an elegant growth habit, this plant is a favorite for bonsai landscapes. I find it likes a fair amount of water, so I tend to grow it in boggy conditions. It prefers shade but will tolerate sun, and it likes moist, well-drained soil.

Prunus serrulata 'Kwanzan'

This cherry tree flowers for just a few weeks each year, when its pink flowers create a spectacular display. Cherry trees benefit from an annual dressing of lime. To get the best flowering, protect it from wind. It likes a humus-rich, moist, well-drained soil.

Punica granatum

This tree's common name is pomegranate. When grown from a cutting, it will flower after just a few years. It can grow in temperate climates and thrives in warm climates. Tolerant of heat, wind, and alkaline soil, it must be protected from cold in winter. It likes coarse-textured soil.

Punica granatum 'Nana'

For summer color, try this pomegranate with lovely orange flowers that appear without fail every year. It can grow in temperate climates and thrives in warm climates. Tolerant of heat, wind, and alkaline soil, it must be protected from cold in winter. It likes coarse organic soil.

Rhododendron impeditum

Its glossy green foliage; linear, thin trunk; and tiny, mauve flowers make this tree ideal for bonsai. It likes light, well-drained soil that must be acidic. Take care to shelter it from wind. Too much shade will produce poor flowering; too much sun is also harmful, especially in winter.

Rhododendron intricatum

This plant has small blue flowers and tiny leaves. For bonsai it is best to use cuttings, because a plant with developed roots will need too large a planting hole. It prefers cool conditions and likes light, well-drained, acidic soil. Too much shade produces poor flowering; too much sun is also harmful, especially in winter.

Saxifraga cochlearis

This is a beautiful alpine with dainty rosettes of delicate, blue-green leaves. It looks very attractive planted along the side of a rock. Every year, the planting will increase in size, so prune it as needed to keep it in bounds. Saxifrage likes neutral to slightly alkaline, very well-drained soil. Keep it in sun or partial shade.

Schoenoplectus lacustris subsp. tabernaemontani 'Zebrinus'

Zebra rush is a miniature, reedlike grass that can be bought in aquarium supply stores as well as at garden centers. Its linear structure adds movement to a background and provides perspective. Keep the soil moist at all times. It likes sun or light shade.

Schoenoplectus tabernaemontani

An erect grass, *S. tabernaemontani* is a weed in many gardens. I use it in my landscapes to exaggerate linear planting, as I find it gives an exciting lift to a landscape. Keep the soil moist at all times. It likes sun or light shade.

Sedum album 'Coral Carpet'

I plant this alpine with rich, fleshy, green-purple foliage at the base of rocks so that they appear to protrude from the ground. It likes moist soil with good drainage and loves full sun. It will tolerate partial shade or heat, as well as drought and poor soil.

Sedum hispanicum

In spring, the network of delicate branches on this blue alpine takes on an arid appearance. Transplant the specimen from gravel paths in spring, not summer, or it will die. It loves full sun and does best in loamy, well-drained soil.

Sedum spathulifolium 'Cape Blanco'

The plump blue leaves of this sedum are useful for providing a change in ground texture. In summer, bright yellow flowers contrast with the leaves. It needs well-drained soil and tolerates partial shade.

Selaginella kraussiana

A fast-growing, mossy fern, this plant makes a good ground cover alternative to moss, as it is thicker and denser in structure. To keep it from overpowering a landscape, break off pieces from the parent plant. It likes full sun and prefers moist, peaty soil.

Sempervivum tectorum

Commonly known as hens-and-chicks, this plant provides richly colored carpets of foliage. Choose plants with small rosettes. Sempervivum prefers full sun, and its soil should be dry to moist.

Thymus x citriodorus

This lovely lemon-scented variety of the culinary herb has woody stems. I use its light-colored foliage to give an illusion of sunshine; its dense growth makes it ideal in a design. It likes full sun and loose, sandy or rocky soil with excellent drainage; it will rot in moist to wet soils.

Thymus serpyllum 'Elfin'

I use this thyme variety to represent low-growing foliage when I need to cover a large area. Its purple-green color creates an illusion of depth. This variety thrives in loose, sandy or rocky soil with good drainage. It likes full sun and tolerates drought and poor soil.

Thymus vulgaris

Any species of thyme is suitable for bonsai landscapes. I use common thyme for its bushy form and dull, mid-green leaves. Whorls of tiny tubular lilac flowers appear in late spring. It likes loose, sandy or rocky soil with excellent drainage and does best in full sun.

Ulmus parvifolia

Better known as Chinese elm, this is a durable and hardy tree. Grown outside, the bark develops a yellow tinge, and in fall the leaves turn pink. Small-leaved varieties are best for bonsai. It tolerates cool conditions outdoors and hot, dry conditions indoors. It likes light and sun and a rich, moist soil with full drainage.

Viola sylvestris

This dainty wood violet, known as wood dog violet, has lovely, delicately scented purple flowers in spring. Wood violet is an invasive plant that self-seeds readily; be sure to pinch off the flowers before they go to seed. It likes partial to full shade. Keep the soil moist at all times.

GLOSSARY

akadama
Baked potting clay from Japan. The coarse grade is used for drainage, the medium grade is used for general potting, and the fine grade is used on the surface to encourage the growth of moss.

bonsai pad
A dense fibrous pad formed from sedge peat and tree roots. The formation of a pad allows the bonsai tree to be moved without being damaged.

bonsai soil mix
A soil mix consisting of one part loam, two parts sphagnum moss, and two parts granite grit.

bonsai wire
Traditionally copper, but now more usually anodized aluminum. Used for shaping trunks and branches.

broom style
A method of pruning aimed at producing a tree that resembles a Japanese broom.

ciment fondu
A very fine cement that sets on contact with water. It is used in the construction of artificial rocks.

clip-and-grow method
A technique of cutting back branches and allowing new branches to form before cutting back again. Produces an aged appearance quite quickly.

clump style
A method of training to create the effect of multiple trunks growing from a single root.

culm
The jointed stem of bamboo or other grass. In bonsai, the culm is peeled in order to slow down growth.

driftwood style
A method of peeling the bark to create the effect of deadwood, or driftwood.

ericaceous soil
An acidic soil mix that is used mainly for azaleas; an alkaline (lime) soil mix would kill them.

exposed-root style
A method of training that encourages part of the root system to grow above the soil.

feng shui
The Chinese practice whereby a place is harmonized with the spiritual energy that flows through it.

foliage pad
A cushion of foliage on the upper side of a branch, created by pruning. Known in Chinese as "steps to heaven."

formal upright style
In this style, the trunk is straight and the tree tapers toward the top.

group planting
A technique for planting several trees in a group so that they share a single bonsai pad.

informal upright style
The most common bonsai style. In this style, the trunk is upright but has some curves.

internode
The length of stem that is found between two leaf joints.

jin
A dead branch, or driftwood. The effect of *jin* can be created artificially in bonsai.

literati style
A method of training that results in a trunk with free-flowing curves, dramatic twists, and a small number of expressive branches.

octopus style
Similar to informal upright style, but with more exaggerated curves and twists.

penjing
A Chinese term literally meaning "landscape in a pot or dish." An older form of bonsai, *penjing* is the art of creating miniature scenes.

planting pockets
Sedge peat molded into pockets in which tree roots are buried to form the bonsai pad.

raft style
A method of training a single tree so that its branches produce the effect of several trees growing in a group.

root-clasped-to-rock style
A method of training that produces the effect of exposed roots clinging to rock.

root-on-rock style
A more advanced variation of the root-clasped-to-rock style, involving the slow and painstaking exposure of roots over a period of years.

semicascade style
A method of training a tree to grow horizontally or near horizontally, which produces the effect of a tree hanging over the edge of a cliff.

suiban
A baked clay water tray traditionally made in Japan.

training box
A deep box used to develop the long roots that are necessary for certain bonsai styles.

twin-trunk style
A method of training two trees to grow with their root systems entwined to form a single bonsai pad.

yin and yang
In Chinese cosmology, the feminine and masculine principles that combine to produce everything that exists.

INDEX

RESOURCES

MAGAZINES

Bonsai
Bonsai Clubs International
P.O. Box 8445
Metairie, LA 70011–8445
(504) 832–8071
www.bonsai-bci.com

Bonsai Today
Stone Lantern Publishing Co.
P.O. Box 324
Watertown, MA 02471
(800) 776–1167
(617) 926–2121
www.stonelantern.com

International Bonsai
International Bonsai Arboretum
P.O. Box 23894
Rochester, NY 14692–3894
(585) 334–2595
www.internationalbonsai.com

SUPPLIERS

Bonsai Boy of New York
555 North Country Road
St. James, NY 11780
(800) 790–2763
www.bonsaiboy.com

Bonsai Collectables
43840 Victor Place
Lancaster, CA 93535
(661) 946–0762
www.bonsai-collectables.com

Bonsai by the Monastery
2625 Highway 212 SW
Conyers, GA 30094
(800) 778–7687
www.bonsaimonk.com

Bonsai Nursery Inc.
3750 S. Federal Boulevard
Englewood, CO 80110
(303) 761–3066

Bonsai West
100 Great Road; P.O. Box 1291
Littleton, MA 01460
(978) 486–3556
www.bonsaiwest.com

Brussel's Bonsai Nursery
8365 Center Hill Road
Olive Branch, MS 38654
(800) 582–2593
www.brusselsbonsai.com

DuPont Bonsai
95865 McKinnon Drive

Gold Beach, OR 97444
(541) 247–9114

International Bonsai Arboretum
P.O. Box 23894
Rochester, NY 14692–3894
(585) 334–2595
www.internationalbonsai.com

Matsu Momiji Nursery
7520 Troy Stone Drive
Fuquay Varina, NC 27526
(919) 552–2592
www.matsumomiji.com

Miami Tropical Bonsai
14775 SW 232nd Street
Miami, FL 33170
(305) 258–0865
www.miamitropicalbonsai.com

New England Bonsai Gardens, Inc.
914 South Main Street (Rt. 126)
Bellingham, MA 02019–1846
(800) 845–0456
www.nebonsai.com

Plant City Bonsai
5607 Cleveland Highway (129N)
Clermont, GA 30527
(770) 983–3377
www.plantcitybonsai.com

Shanti Bithi Nursery
3047 High Ridge Road
Stamford, CT 06903
(203) 329–0768
www.shantibithi.com

Shikoku Bonsai
RR 24 2530 Miles
British Columbia, Canada V0N 2W4
(604) 886–3915
www.shikoku.ca

Wildwood Gardens
14488 Rock Creek Road
Chardon, OH 44024
(440) 286–3714
www.wildwoodgardens.com

ORGANIZATIONS

The American Bonsai Society
P.O. Box 351604
Toledo, OH 43635–1604
www.absbonsai.org

Bonsai Clubs International
P.O. Box 8445
Metairie, LA 70011–8445
(504) 832–8071
www.bonsai-bci.com

CREDITS

The author wishes to thank:
Mark Mills, for his invaluable help in transporting landscapes to and from photography shoots. Bill Brown, for his handmade tray, used in Gong Ji Shan (page 36). Susan Collins, for the loan of Feng Hong (page 48) and her constant supply of lush moss. Adrian Mott, for all the years of encouragement and support.